alibris

TOP NOTCH BOOKS
8801 HWY. 377 W
TOLAR, TX 76476
UNITED STATES

To: ALIBRIS APEX DC 76670938-91
APEX
800 AVONDALE AVE.
GRANDVIEW HEIGHTS, OH 43212-3473

Shipping Instructions for TOPNOTCH

Print this Packing Slip and enclose inside the front cover of the book.

Please ship this item no later than Fri Aug 14, 2026.

Ship to:

ALIBRIS APEX DC 76670938-91
APEX
800 AVONDALE AVE.
GRANDVIEW HEIGHTS, OH 43212-3473
UNITED STATES

PN #	Item ID	Alibris ID	Media Type	Title / Author	Seller List Price	Order Date
76670938-91	044663	B083907064	BOOK	Buying Your Own Small Business Smith, Brian R.; West, Thomas L.	$10.00	Aug, 4 2026

Good. No Jacket Folio-over 12"-15" tall. Hard Cover Cover is bumped and scuffed. Pages are clean and tight.

76670938-91

YOUR THREE-YEAR BUSINESS PLAN FOR BUYING A SMALL BUSINESS

Detach this booklet by tearing along perforation in back cover.

Your Three-Year Business Plan for Buying a Small Business
This workbook is an integral part of *Buying Your Own Small Business*.

First published in 1985 by The Stephen Greene Press, Inc.
Published simultaneously in Canada by Penguin Books Canada Limited
Distributed by Viking Penguin Inc., 40 West 23rd Street,
New York, New York 10010

Printed in the United States of America by
Hamilton Printing Company, Rensselaer, New York
Designed by Irving Perkins Associates

BUSINESS PLAN FOR

____

(insert name of business)

Prepared by:
Date:

SUMMARY

(1. Give the name of the business, its location, and description of its physical facilities.)

(2. Briefly describe the product or service.)

(3. What market—consumer, industrial, government—are you serving? What segment of that market—teenagers, adult males—are you serving? What is unique about this business?)

(4. What are the overall goals of the business? Who are the people connected with the business?)

PURPOSE

The purpose of this prospectus is

TABLE OF CONTENTS

(Fill this in after the plan has been completed. Be certain to show page numbers if the plan runs to more than 15 pages.)

I. THE BUSINESS

A. *Business Description*

1. Name

2. Location

3. Physical Facilities

4. Business History (optional)

B. *Products or Services*

1. Description of Product Line

(Use more pages if necessary.)

2. Proprietary Considerations

C. *Management Plan*

1. Organizational Form and Structure

2. Résumés of Key People

3. Staffing Plan

4. Supporting Services

Attorney:

Accountant:

Consultant:

Insurance Agent:

Advertising Agency:

D. *Operations Plan*

1. Facilities and Equipment

2. Plans For Growth and Expansion

3. Overall Schedule

4. Process Description

E. *Risks*

1.

2.

3.

4.

5.

II. MARKETING PLAN

A. *Marketing Research*

1. Description of the Market.

2. Industry Trends.

3. Target Market.

4. Competition.
   Competitor #1.

   Competitor #2.

   Competitor #3.

(Use more sheets if necessary.)

B. *Objectives and Strategy*

C. *Pricing Policy*

D. *Sales Terms*

E. *Method of Sales and Distribution*

F. *Customer Service*

G. *Advertising and Promotion*

H. *Forecasts*

III. FINANCIAL DATA

A. *Proposal*

(Center this on a single page.)

B. *Source and Use of Funds*

Sources of Funds

1.

2.

3.

4.

Use of Proceeds

1.

2.

3.

4.

5.

6.

7.

8.

C. *Historical Financial Statements*

(Past three years' income statements and balance sheets; tax returns if statements are unavailable.)

D. *Cash Flow Projections*

Acquisition Costs and Beginning Cash

1. Inventory	$________
2. Deposits	
a. Rent	________
b. Utilities, telephone	________
c. Sales tax	________
d. Other (specify):	________
3. Fees	
a. Professional (legal, accounting)	________
b. Licenses, permits, taxes	________
c. Other (specify):	________
4. Decorating, remodeling, repairs	________
5. Closing costs	________
6. Insurance	________
7. Miscellaneous	________
TOTAL COSTS	$________
BEGINNING CASH	$________

(Use the space below for any explanations about the cash flow projections.)

E. *Pro Forma Income Statements*

(Use the space below for explanations, comments.)

PRO FORMA INCOME STATEMENT

Business ____________________

Period ____________________

		%
Net Sales	$	
Cost of Goods Sold		
	______	___
Gross Margin	$	
Expenses		
Payroll expense	$	
Outside services		
Business supplies		
Repairs and maintenance		
Advertising		
Car, delivery, travel		
Accounting and legal		
Rent		
Telephone and utilities		
Insurance		
Taxes		
Equipment rental		
Depreciation		
Postage and printing		
Interest		
Miscellaneous		
Other (specify):		
Total Expenses	______	___
Profit (Loss) before tax	$	
Federal and State tax (%)	______	___
Profit after tax	$	

F. *Breakeven Analysis*

IV. APPENDICES

Buying Your Own Small Business

Buying Your Own Small Business

BRIAN R. SMITH
THOMAS L. WEST

THE STEPHEN GREENE PRESS • LEXINGTON, MASSACHUSETTS

First published in 1985 by The Stephen Greene Press, Inc.
Published simultaneously in Canada by Penguin Books Canada Limited
Distributed by Viking Penguin Inc., 40 West 23rd Street,
New York, New York 10010

LIBRARY OF CONGRESS CATALOGING IN PUBLICATION DATA
Smith, Brian R., 1939–
Buying your own small business.
1. Small business—Management. 2. Self-employed.
I. West, Thomas L., 1936– . II. Title.
HD62.7.S62 1984 658.1'141 84-19390
ISBN 0-86616-047-7

Printed in the United States of America by
Hamilton Printing Company, Rensselaer, New York
Designed by Irving Perkins Associates

Acknowledgments

We wish to thank four fine people who helped us to put this book together: Beth Love, who helped to be sure that manuscript material changed hands between us at the right times; Susan Patterson, who typed some original work; Marjorie A. Zerbel, who typed the entire final manuscript; and Myrna M. Milani, who edited the material before it went to typing.

To my father, Ray West, who always wanted to write a book; to my father-in-law, Russ Wright, who gave me the knowledge to write the book; and to my wife, Barbara, who inspired me to write the book.

T L W

In loving memory of my parents, Elmer and Jessie Smith.

B R S

Contents

Introduction

No one knows for sure the number of businesses sold every year, but it may be in the millions. Although this figure includes acquisitions of one multi-billion-dollar, multi-national corporation by another, the vast majority of businesses changing hands are small operations grossing less than $250,000 annually. As a business becomes larger, the procedures involved in its purchase become more complex; the sale of a large corporation requires roomfuls of lawyers, accountants, acquisition specialists and tax advisors, and stockholder approval as well. Governmental agencies such as the Securities and Exchange Commission may become involved. Financing may take several forms and the period of negotiation may take months and cost hundreds of thousands of dollars. Compare this to the purchase (and sale) of Happy Herman's Pizza and Sub Shoppe, grossing around $100,000 a year, which occurs after a few hours' discussion between the business owner or seller and the buyer.

The successful purchase of a large business requires the satisfaction of specific legal and financial criteria *and* a proper methodology. The same should be true with the purchase of smaller operations, but too often small business buyers fail to use any methodology at all beyond the most rudimentary approach. Consequently, people buy the wrong kind of business in relation to their lifestyle, likes, and dislikes; or they pay too much for a business, get trapped in a set of restrictive conditions, or even purchase a business with a fatal flaw hidden somewhere under the surface. We're not suggesting you go through the same buying procedures used by large corporations. However, we do suggest you follow some basic steps and analyses that lead to successful business ownership.

This is a book about the right way to *buy* a small business; it's not a book about how to *start* a business from scratch. If you're a true entrepreneur and aren't sure you'll be satisfied with a used business, you may also want to read *Raising Seed Money For Your Own Business* (Brian R. Smith, The Lewis Publishing Co., 1984). Although there are some similarities between buying and starting a business, there are significant differences in the two approaches to self-employment you should know about before you make any final decisions.

This book gives you a simple, step-by-step method for buying a business. We've both been in and around small business for a combined period of over 40 years and we've seen all the mistakes—the big ones, anyway. What we're giving you is based on our experience of personally observing and being involved in the sale of hundreds of businesses of all sizes and types.

The proposed methodology works for almost any size business purchase but we emphasize its use for acquiring a business doing less than a quarter of a million dollars in sales per year. Also, we speak primarily about what we call normal businesses—dress shops, motels, small restaurants—those having uncomplicated legal and financial structures. We don't discuss the purchase of businesses having special market potential (such as young, high-technology ventures) or corporations with many stockholders which require special care and handling. Essentially our method is for the purchase of smaller, less complex businesses where most of the work can and should be done by you. We don't rule out the use of professionals—accountants, attorneys, consultants—but you need to do most of the homework yourself because it's going to be your business.

Brian R. Smith
Thomas L. West

Chapter ONE

The Basics of Small Business Ownership

WHO WANTS TO OWN A SMALL BUSINESS?

Very few people get into their own business right after high school or college, primarily because it's easier to get a job than buy or start a business. Being an employee also has other advantages: a regular paycheck, employer-paid benefits, the opportunity to try your wings, even make a few mistakes with relatively few risks. If you make an outlandish boo-boo at Engulf and Devour, the worst thing that can happen is you'll be fired, which may not be all that bad anway. If you make a similar error in your own business, you may very well lose everything you own. Finally, few young people have the necessary capital to buy a business or support themselves until a new business venture becomes profitable. True, some fresh out of high school or college have the necessary family financial backing to start or buy a business, but those individuals are rare.

In general, people who buy businesses first spend a number of years as a hired hand. Some begin their career as an employee knowing full well they eventually want to be self-employed. Others discover after 5, 15, or 25 years of working for someone else, that they want to chart their own course; at this point they leave the womb of employment and strike out on their own. Still other potential business owners wait until retirement. The patterns are many and varied, and no one pattern guarantees success. The key is timing; become self-employed when you're ready and feel right about it. Become self-employed because you want it and for no other reason. We see too many people get into business for wrong reasons like:

- they believe they'll get rich
- they believe they'll gain great prestige
- they're trying to show off—to a former employer, a former spouse, a mother-in-law
- they're escaping, running away from something.

To be sure, business ownership can bring fame and fortune, but these are by-products, not primary aims.

When you're an employee, and given things like a paycheck and a place to work, you're expected to do things in return—come to work at a certain time, perfrom certain duties, agree to abide by certain policies. Your advancement is largely in the hands of other people. For many, this is an acceptable, even desirable way of life. To them, it's comforting to know the paycheck will be there every Thursday; they don't even have to think about it. For some, however, the agreements that an employee must abide by aren't palatable and they prefer to create their own work in their own way; they choose to become self-employed.

There are other differences between being employed and self-employed to be aware of so you choose the form of your life's work that's best for you. Once you make the proper choice, you'll have no reason to look back in regret. We're *not* saying there's anything wrong with working for an employer any more than we *are* saying the entrepreneurial route is the right one for everyone.

Ten times more Americans are employed than self-employed. We don't know if *every* employed person thinks about being in business for him or herself, but certainly the majority do at one time or another. After all, self-employment's the Great American Dream—even more so than a second car. Even the Fortune 500 corporations, with hundreds of thousands of employees, worldwide operations, and billions of dollars in assets, probably began as an entrepreneurial venture, springing from the drive and imagination of a single individual. As a society, we extol the virtues of creativity, independence, ambition, self-reliance; and we admire the man or woman with these characteristics who does it independently.

For every 100 employed people who dream about getting into their own business, only 1 or 2 actually do it. Those who don't may be afraid of failure or even success, but we also suspect many merely become unnecessarily overwhelmed by the process of becoming self-employed. It doesn't have to be that way. For example, there are only three ways to become self-employed:

1. Start a business.
2. Buy an existing business.
3. Buy a franchise.

Each of these requires its own methodology which, when followed, drastically reduces the probability of business failure. This book provides a methodology for buying an existing business, although we will discuss franchises later.

Regardless of what route you're considering, bear in mind that there's a big difference between working for someone else and working for yourself. Don't rush into it. Don't do it because it's a job of last resort. If you need the paycheck, the benefits, the structure, and the policies created by an employer, then by all means, don't give them up. We have both had people come up to us in our seminars and thank us for helping them preserve their life savings—whether it was $5,000 or $500,000—because we helped them realize business ownership was not for them. To be in your own business and be successful, you must

- forget, once and for all, that anyone will provide anything *for* you. You must provide for *yourself.*
- remember that you create your reality.
- recognize that you choose self-employment as a result of what you want, not because it's the last course open to you.
- believe that there is a need for the kind of business you want to be in.
- know you can do whatever you want as long as "whatever" is what you truly want to do.
- shake off any beliefs you have about "The Right Stuff" regarding what education, experience, or background is required to be successfully self-employed.
- see business ownership as a way to express yourself to the world, not a way to manipulate it.
- want to succeed to retain the self-pride and awareness that you can indeed do it on your own.
- have fun, enjoy solving problems, and want to help others.

STARTING VERSUS BUYING A BUSINESS

There are some people who cannot be satisfied with the purchase of a going concern. These are the true entrepreneurs—those who, for their own reasons, must create a business from scratch. Others who seek self-employment would never dream of such a venture. There are advantages and disadvantages to both of these routes to consider before proceeding in either direction. Here are some of the differences between the two approaches:

1. When you buy a business, almost everything you need is already in place, from an established clien-

tele to a business telephone, to the name of the business. When you start a business, everything must be created, but that also means you can tailor it exactly to your needs. Of course, an established business can be changed to fit the style of the new owner, but sometimes these changes can harm the business rather than help it.
2. A business can be started quickly or allowed to evolve over a number of years. This gives the owner the opportunity to learn and grow with the business. When you buy a business, you must initially learn as much about the business in as short a time as possible because it continues to operate and evolve at the former rate.
3. It's usually cheaper to buy a business than create that same business from scratch. That's because an entrepreneur does many things in the early years of the business he or she is never fully paid for: building a reputation, establishing a market, hiring employees.
4. It's easier to find financing for a business acquisition than a startup. Seller financing to one degree or another is usually available for business acquisition.
5. The risk of failure is much higher with startups. There's no exact data available, but we estimate only two out of every ten businesses started last five years; of every ten businesses purchased, at least eight survive.
6. The going concern has a proven track record. It already does what a business should do—offers a product or service to a group of customers and makes a profit. No such evidence exists for the startup.
7. It takes more skill and energy to create a successful business from a startup.

However, the most important difference between those who start and those who buy a business has to do with personal style and the characteristics of the potential business owner.

If we construct a scale based on an arbitrary system of one to ten, where ten represents the maximum entrepreneurial rating, we may categorize the entire spectrum as shown below.

This spectrum demonstrates the balance between two variables—the need for security and the need for independence. It doesn't show that entrepreneurs are better than government employees; it simply indicates that their needs are different. Where do you place yourself on the spectrum?

ARE BUSINESS OWNERS DIFFERENT?

Many people, including the two of us, study entrepreneurs and small business owners in relation to their counterparts who work for someone else. The following 20 questions are designed to help you assess yourself in terms of some of those qualities characteristic of successful business owners. Be brutally honest while taking this quiz; otherwise it's meaningless and may even lead you to make an unwise decision regarding your future type of employment.

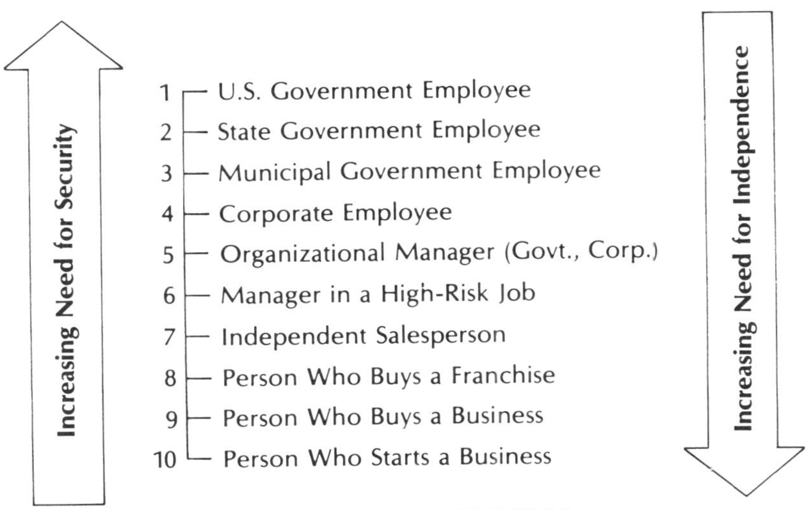

ENTREPRENEURIAL SPECTRUM

1. Are you willing to take moderate risks in life to achieve the goals you want? (Please note the use of the word *moderate*. Business owners are not gamblers.)
   ☐ Yes
   ☐ No
   ☐ Uncertain
2. Can you operate within an environment that is somewhat ill-defined and may, from time to time, even be chaotic?
   ☐ Yes
   ☐ No
   ☐ Uncertain
3. Do you possess the drive and energy to work long hours to achieve what you want?
   ☐ Yes
   ☐ No
   ☐ Uncertain
4. Are you prepared to place the needs of your business above those of your friends, your family, your community?
   ☐ Yes
   ☐ No
   ☐ Uncertain
5. Are you the kind of person who can take full responsibility for both your successes and your failures?
   ☐ Yes
   ☐ No
   ☐ Uncertain
6. Are failures merely learning experiences to you?
   ☐ Yes
   ☐ No
   ☐ Uncertain
7. Do you need to be in control of your working environment?
   ☐ Yes
   ☐ No
   ☐ Uncertain
8. Are you comfortable around strangers?
   ☐ Yes
   ☐ No
   ☐ Uncertain
9. Can you say "no" to someone you believe is trying to get you to do something you don't want to do?
   ☐ Yes
   ☐ No
   ☐ Uncertain
10. When the need arises, can you tackle and complete a job that may not interest you?
    ☐ Yes
    ☐ No
    ☐ Uncertain
11. Are you willing to work hard to acquire new skills?
    ☐ Yes
    ☐ No
    ☐ Uncertain
12. Can you lead and inspire others?
    ☐ Yes
    ☐ No
    ☐ Uncertain
13. Can you take harsh criticism, even on a personal level?
    ☐ Yes
    ☐ No
    ☐ Uncertain
14. Are you able to hold on to your ideas and ideals even in the face of mass opinion counter to what you believe?
    ☐ Yes
    ☐ No
    ☐ Uncertain

For the next six statements, check the box that reflects your feelings.

15. It's more important to accomplish what I want than earn a great deal of money.
    ☐ Agree
    ☐ Disagree
    ☐ Uncertain
16. People learn more from mistakes than from successes.
    ☐ Agree
    ☐ Disagree
    ☐ Uncertain

17. "Slow and steady wins the race."
- ☐ Agree
- ☐ Disagree
- ☐ Uncertain

18. It's not necessary to cut corners or compromise in order to succeed.
- ☐ Agree
- ☐ Disagree
- ☐ Uncertain

19. I value intangible qualities like love and wisdom over money and possessions.
- ☐ Agree
- ☐ Disagree
- ☐ Uncertain

20. There is no other person I would rather be than me at this moment.
- ☐ Agree
- ☐ Disagree
- ☐ Uncertain

To score this self-assessment, give five points for every "Yes" or "Agree", three points for "Uncertain" and zero for "No" or "Disagree." (Your total score will be between 0 and 100.) Now give yourself a letter grade:

90–100:	A
80–89:	B
70–79:	C
60–69:	D
below 60:	F

Before going on, we want to comment on two qualities of successful business owners that run counter to popular belief. One of these involves money and the other risk-taking. Much of the general public views entrepreneurs as individuals who take inordinately high risks and are only in business to make lots of money. Both views are wrong. True entrepreneurs don't play the game if they feel the odds of the house are against them. Regarding money: small business owners must understand economic values because ours is a free enterprise system, but they know it's far better to make money a measure of progress rather than an end in itself. Your heart is where your true treasure is. If you focus only on money, you may fall victim to bottom-line performance at all costs, forgetting your personal fulfillment and a commitment to serve others.

WHAT IS A SMALL BUSINESS?

If you ask 100 people what a small business is, you get 100 different answers—and all of the answers are right. However, in order to begin considering all the ins and outs of buying a small business, we need a reliable definition. Let's look at the most common definitions and their sources and see if they fit our needs.

Sometimes small businesses are defined in terms of comparisons. For example, a business may be small in the eyes of a seller, but that same business may be a large one in the eyes of a buyer. To IBM, a business selling for $10 million is a small business. To an individual seeking to raise the ten million to buy that business, it's a very large business indeed. There aren't too many of us who can swing that one—even with a small downpayment. Let's look at some other ways people tend to view businesses in terms of size.

- Data General is small compared to IBM.
- Post cereals is small compared to Kellogg.
- Don's Pizza is the largest pizza place in town.
- American Motors is considered a small car manufacturing business with its 28,000 employees.
- General Electric sells fewer televisions than RCA.

Those comparisons don't really help us either, but surely the U.S. government's Small Business Administration can give us the correct definition. Depending on whom you talk to in the Small Business Administration, there are anywhere from 1.7 million to over 17 million small businesses in this country. It makes you wonder who's counting and what they're counting!

A small business located in a college town provided a roommate service for the students who lived off campus. The owner operated out of a spartan 10 x 10 office—with desk, file cabinet and battery of phones. His advertising was limited to local and campus newspapers, yet he made a substantial profit year after year. We wonder if he was part of the Small Business Administration's 1.7 million or even 17 million count; but there he was, year after year, making a tidy profit.

This is just one example of the thousands upon thousands of businesses never recognized by government agencies as a business, but there they are nonetheless—thriving, profitable small businesses. In the SBA's desire to have their agency include all businesses, regardless of size, they claim that approximately 98 percent of all businesses are small businesses. Is that 98 percent of 1.7 million, 17 million, or some number between the two?

For business loan purposes, the SBA defines a small business as one that is independently owned and operated, not dominant in its field, and meets their employment or sales standards. Let's take a look at these standards:

Manufacturing—A small business may have as many as 1,500 employees, depending on the industry in which the applicant is primarily engaged.

Wholesaling—Yearly sales of a small business cannot exceed 9.5 million to 22 million dollars, depending on the industry.

Services—Annual receipts cannot exceed 2 million to 8 million dollars, depending on the industry in which the applicant is primarily engaged.

Retailing—Annual sales or receipts cannot exceed 2 million to 7.5 million dollars, depending on the industry.

Construction—General construction: average annual receipts cannot exceed 9.5 million dollars for the three most recently completed fiscal years. Special trade construction: average annual receipts cannot exceed 1 or 2 million dollars for the three last fiscal years, depending on the industry.

Agriculture—Annual receipts cannot exceed 1 million dollars.

If these criteria are met, the SBA considers the business a small one.

The SBA so often talks of small business in sales of millions and numbers of employees in the hundreds that Mom's three-employee Ice Cream Store doesn't even come close to their definition. In all fairness, the government is trained to think big—so big that the $100,000 or so that Mom's store grosses yearly hardly ranks it as a small business at all. Is this a reasonable orientation? Is this the way it really is?

Let's take a look at reality as we see it:

- Over 50 percent of the businesses in this country have four or fewer employees.
- 92 percent of the businesses in this country have annual sales of $300,000 or less.
- Approximately 90 percent of the businesses in this country have ten or fewer employees.

Your local main street is full of businesses that have fewer than ten employees. In fact, the majority of you will be looking at businesses that have four or fewer employees. That's Main Street America; that's American small business. Let's take our definition one step further:

- A small business is one that supports no more than two families and most likely only one family.

Now that we have defined a small business in terms of its number of employees, annual sales, and ability to support no more than two families, let's add one more qualification to our definition that's of particular interest to you as a potential small business buyer: its price.

Sellers put prices on businesses when they offer them for sale; but, let's face it, the real value of a business is only what someone is willing to pay for it. It's really the old saying, "Beauty is in the eyes of the beholder." Consequently, we can add this to our definition of a small business:

- Its price is determined by the buyer.

By determining how much buyers are willing to spend, we can then define small businesses in terms of selling price. For example, in our opinion, 90 percent of those who buy or plan to buy a business have $50,000 or less to spend, and most have a *lot* less. This amount may be in the form of equity in a house, personal property, retirement funds, or stock. We use a formula that says ideally your down payment is one-third or less of the full purchase price and, we hope, a lot less. Using our formula, we can then say most businesses must sell for $150,000 or less as a *full purchase price* including inventory to appeal to a good portion of the buying public. If most buyers have $50,000 or less as a down payment, then three times this amount is the approximate full purchase price. We can also say that by our definition, a small business is one selling for $150,000 or less.

Let's put a little more emphasis on the *less,* because the majority of businesses sold each year sell for less than $75,000. In fact, a 1982 random sampling of some 1,500 businesses sold nationwide by a major business brokerage firm revealed that:

- 31 percent of these businesses had a full purchase price of $25,000 or less
- 26 percent had a full purchase price of $25,000 to $50,000

- 26 percent had a full purchase price of $50,000 to $75,000
- 5 percent had a full purchase price of $75,000 to $100,000
- 12 percent had a full purchase price in excess of $100,000.

Eighty-three percent of the businesses sold in this sampling had a full purchase price of $75,000 or less. *That's* the kind of small business purchase we want to talk about.

Let's look at what that same sampling showed about down payments:

- 7 percent of those businesses sold with a down payment of $5,000 or less
- 3 percent sold with a down payment of $5,000 to $10,000
- 20 percent sold with a down payment of $10,000 to $20,000
- 14 percent sold with a down payment of $20,000 to $25,000
- 14 percent sold with a down payment of $25,000 to $30,000
- 16 percent sold with a down payment of $30,000 to $40,000
- 9 percent sold with a down payment of $40,000 to $50,000
- 17 percent sold with a down payment in excess of $75,000.

Almost one-half of the businesses sold had a down payment of $30,000 or less, and 71 percent of the businesses sold had a down payment of $50,000 or less.

What does all this mean to you as a potential small business buyer? First, if you add up the total selling price of all the businesses sold last year and divide it by the number sold, you get an average sale price of $75,000, $5,000 less than that of the average home. Although the financial pages of the local newspapers are filled with business mergers, acquisitions, and takeovers, the sale of Mom's Ice Cream Store never makes the financial news.

Secondly, there are 230,000,000 people in this country and 15,000,000 small businesses; that's one business for every 15 people. If the majority of these businesses sell for $75,000 or less, there are over eight million businesses for you to choose from. Of these, approximately 25 percent, almost 2,000,000, change hands each year. That's quite a few small businesses for you to consider. One final statistic about our average small business: It has gross sales of $250,000 or less a year and should provide the owner with a comfortable living.

Now that we've defined the kind of business we're talking about, let's look at some myths that hamper would-be buyers.

MYTHS ABOUT SMALL BUSINESS AND OWNERSHIP

Many people never get into their own business because they have false assumptions about what it takes to be self-employed or they believe certain negative consequences are inevitable. Others create reasons to talk themselves out of what they want. Here are some common myths we'd like to dispel.

Myth	Reality
1. Most people get into business to make lots of money.	1. Most people get into business because they can't work (or aren't working) for someone else.
2. To be successful, you must be unethical.	2. Most small businesses are run by ethical people.
3. It's nearly impossible to acquire the necessary skills to run your own business.	3. Millions of others have clearly done it. The skills are learnable.
4. There are many outside factors waiting to cripple a small business. For example, a large business can bury a small one.	4. Businesses fail because the owner does not act or react properly. Big businesses don't have the time or interest to bury a small business.
5. If I fail, I'm ruined.	5. Many business owners fail before they succeed. The failure merely becomes a learning experience.
6. My family won't support me.	6. If they realize it's something that's very important to you, they'll probably support you wholeheartedly.
7. It's a lot of hard work.	7. Most successful business owners don't see it that way—for them it's more play than work.
8. It takes a lot of money to buy a small business.	8. It takes a lot of money to buy a *big* business.

There's one and only one real test of your suitability to own a business—you must want it because it is the right thing for you. If it's a desperation move because you lost your job, you'll probably fail. If you're doing it for greed or status, you'll probably fail. If you're doing it because you want to show up a former employer, a former spouse, or a parent, you'll probably also fail.

Let's put this final test in the form of a question: if someone gave you a business ownership, would you take it? Never mind any conditions or reasons. Would you take it?

Chapter TWO

Lifestyle and Business

George got fed up with working for the welfare department of New York City, took early retirement, sold his house, moved to Vermont, and bought a small inn. He believed he was fulfilling his life's dream—his own romantic dream of business in the country. Eighteen months later the inn was on the market and George was ready to go back to the city. What happened? For one thing, George learned being in business for yourself wasn't all it was cracked up to be. In his city job, George worked 36 hours a week, never took work home, and received regular paychecks, promotions, and raises. At the inn, George sometimes worked 18 hours a day. To make matters worse, the inn's income depended heavily on tourism, and last year's snowless winter meant low earnings. George was used to the services of the city and wasn't very handy when it came to fixing the plumbing or the wiring. He was a city boy. To add to the problem, he was not suited to a hospitality business; he really didn't like catering to people. He would have been better off in a service business—and in the city, or at least the suburbs.

The lesson? Give serious thought to *all* the factors before acquiring a business. Let's talk first about geography: Where will you look for this business of yours?

If you live in Peoria and plan to buy a business there, many of the unknowns you face moving to a strange location are eliminated. You already know many things about Peoria, the most important of which is what the people are like. Most first-time buyers acquire a business that depends on local customers (retail, service, hospitality) rather than a manufacturing or wholesaling business whose customers come from everywhere, even other countries.

If you don't stay put, you buy your business somewhere else. Let's give some thought to this "somewhere else" before you go skipping off to places unknown.

YOU CAN'T GO HOME AGAIN

Let's say you grew up in a small rural town in Missouri but moved to Chicago where you've been working for Glutz Industries for the past 15 years. You dream about going back to your home town and maybe even buying that corner drug store where you and your pals used to hang out, the store run by the old man who looked like Papa Gipetto. Your memories are 15 years old; the corner store's been replaced by a 360,000 square foot shopping center. Most of your school chums have moved away, and the closest you can get to the kindly proprietor is to visit his grave site behind St. Bernard's church. Some of your former high school teachers retired or died and those still teaching probably don't remember you.

We aren't saying it's impossible to return home after a lengthy stay elsewhere, but just keep in mind that things won't be the same as when you left. Don't think the old town is going to turn out in full force and give you a ticker-tape parade down Main Street, welcoming home a returning hero from his quests. As a matter of fact, there may even be some resentment to your coming home. "What's the matter—wasn't Chicago good enough for you?"

If you do decide to return, and it's been a number of years since you left, do some research on the old home town. Discover what's changed since you left. The economy may have worsened, especially if some of the larger employers have left or closed shop. The age breakdown or predominant ethnic group you relied on may no longer exist. In many ways it may be harder to re-establish yourself in the town you left than plant your roots in an entirely new area.

COUNTRY, CITY, SUBURBS

It's important to your business success to be where you want to be, so if you're going to move, give thought to your lifestyle as it relates to population density—that factor that determines whether a locale is rural, urban, or suburban. Sometimes the distinction is blurred; most of Wyoming and Montana is obviously rural and Manhattan is certainly urban, but what about a town of 30,000 in the middle of Virginia or Oklahoma? It probably embraces some of the characteristics of all three classifications.

Most people aren't suited to country living. If they were, there would be more people living in the country, and then it wouldn't be the country any more. Rural areas contain two kinds of people: those born there and those who move there, usually for specific reasons. These groups don't generally get along; their views on themselves and the world differ. There may be wealth mixed with poverty, such as a near-mansion standing next to a wood-and-tarpaper shack held together with wire and corrugated, rusted sheet metal. If you plan to buy a rural business like a small grocery or general store that serves the "locals," remember you'll initially be considered an outsider. People will come by slowly to size you up and if you pass muster, you'll eventually be accepted. If you don't, kiss the business good-bye.

Cyrus Blanchard successfully ran a small general store in a New Hampshire town for years. Cy sold the store to a couple from the city. One year later, the couple abandoned the store and the bank picked up the pieces. What happened? Well, Cy wasn't only a smart business owner, he was a wise one; he knew and cared about people. He spent an hour or two every Sunday morning putting townspeople's names on the Sunday editions of the *Boston Globe,* the *Manchester Union-Leader* and *The New York Times* to reserve them. If old Mrs. Chickering came in only once a year to buy a particular kind of mustard, it was on the shelf. You could order a whole cow and Cy would buy it, cut it the way you wanted it, wrap it, and freeze it for you.

The new owners did away with all that frivolousness. They also worked shorter hours; no profit between 6 and 9 P.M., they said. In six months all their customers were tourists. When the tourists at summer's end left, the store folded.

Things go more slowly in the country; that's why most folks live there. You also have fewer services in the country: no trash pick-up, or town water, for example. The power may go out frequently. You might find a pig in your yard some morning. If your house catches fire, it may burn to the ground by the time the volunteer fire department gets there and finds out where to get water for the pumper.

This may sound a bit harsh, but it's all for a good reason: too many folks dream about the peace, serenity, clean air, low taxes, negligible crime, and solitude of the rural life. Yes, it has these things, but there are other factors to consider. The lifestyle is quite different from the suburbs or the city itself. If you're seriously considering purchasing a country business, be sure to read *How To Find and Buy Your Business in the Country* by Frank Kirkpatrick (Garden Way Publishing, 1984).

Now let's look at life in the city. The city is certainly everything the country is not. It's fast, exciting, innovative. There's much to do and there are services of all kinds. City people aren't as patient, and tend to be more sophisticated (whatever that means) and educated than their rural counterparts. Some prospective business owners believe the city is the place to make lots of money. While the need for more business is higher in the city because of the greater population, it also means there is a potential for more competition. Furthermore, costs such as taxes, rent, and insurance are much greater, and crime is often part of everyday life.

However, many cities have made positive moves to clean up slums and re-establish themselves as safe places to live and work. After two decades of declining city populations, there's a trickle of folks returning. During the 1980s and 1990s we may even see a revival of a number of our cities.

The suburbs offer another alternative, but here again, you must be careful. The communities surrounding a city can vary from impoverished to wealthy. There are massive shopping centers with so much foot traffic a business stands a high probability of success, but over-expansion of small businesses is also often a problem. Suburbs undergo lots of changes as people move in and out of them; a single suburban community can change significantly in five years because of the turnover in the population. However, for someone who feels the country is too slow and the city too fast, a suburban business may present the best balance. Most businesses bought and sold are in the suburbs. Because of higher disposable incomes in communities around cities, many potential business owners see the suburbs as a perfect place to start or buy a highly profitable business. These higher incomes also draw in more chains and franchises.

The important thing about location is to be aware of those differences related to geography as well as the kind of environment that best suits your lifestyle. If you plan a significant change like going from the city to the country, be sure to spend some time in your proposed locale before you buy.

WHAT KIND OF BUSINESS SHOULD YOU BUY?

You may think the most difficult decision is whether to buy a business or not, but many times the most important and difficult choice is what kind of business to buy. Here are a few questions to help you in the process.

- Do you want to get up at 3:00 A.M. to make the day's supply of doughnuts?
- Do you want to work until midnight cooking and serving pizza?
- Do you want to work behind a counter selling and waiting on customers in a retail business?
- Do you want to attend to people's needs—as in a service business?
- Do you want to distribute something or manufacture a product?

There are almost as many different businesses as there are people to buy them. So you can let your imagination run wild. What do you want to do? What are your strengths and weaknesses? If you are a klutz when it comes to the mechanical world, then you probably don't want to consider a coin laundry (machines always need repairs—and a professional repair person can eat up all the profits), auto repair, or a fix-it type of business.

Sometimes the right business finds you. How does this happen? Begin by reading the business opportunity section of the Sunday edition of your nearest metropolitan newspaper. Small papers usually don't have such sections, or at best have limited business sections that don't offer the variety and scope you need. Carefully look at the variety of ads. Most papers arrange the business opportunity ads alphabetically. Some ads have franchise and display ads at the top of the page and individual businesses on the bottom two-thirds. Other papers reverse the order. In either case, read all the ads from A to Z. Does anything catch your fancy? Did you notice anything? At least 50 percent of the ads were in the area of food and drink-related businesses, weren't they? From bars or taverns to coffee shops and cocktail lounges, convenience stores, fast-food restaurants, cafés, delis, grocery stores. Sprinkled among all these are the retail and service businesses. Occasionally you may find a small manufacturing company or a route distributorship. Some appeal to you, some don't. If you don't like animals, there's no point looking at pet shops. If you're not mechanically inclined, why bother looking at hardware or auto parts stores?

You may look at all this, especially the food and drink places, and get discouraged because the last thing you want to do is serve ice cream or mix cocktails. However, before you throw the newspaper down in disgust, do some thinking. Remember old Uncle Charlie? He had a liquor store in Bayonne, New Jersey; he also always had a new Cadillac parked in back of the store. How about Aunt Emmy? She owned that coffee shop in some little town in Iowa, and eventually she also owned half the town. Think about all the food places springing up everywhere; main highways seem to be bordered with every type imaginable. Of course, many food places are franchised, but someone owns and runs them, and almost all franchises are independently owned and operated.

Take a good look at the range of food and drink businesses. You don't run out and buy a French restaurant first time around, but you could run an ice cream store, a convenience store, or a fast-food place. Except for the tablecloth type of restaurant, food and drink businesses are easy to run, easy to get into, and generally low risk. Many who ponder the ads end up following through on a food and drink type of business—maybe just out of curiosity, but also just to get started.

WHAT KINDS OF BUSINESSES ARE BOUGHT?

Let's take a look at what kinds of businesses most people buy. You don't have to fit into these patterns, but it may be reassuring to know that other people are buying. Knowing what businesses sell also gives you an indication of what's available. You might think food and drink places sell more than any other business because they don't do as well and therfore are always for sale, but that's not true. Food and drink businesses can be confining, and when the walls start closing in, people want to sell. Also, people with no experience buy those types of businesses for the reasons described earlier, and not everyone who buys a business makes it. However, even a business that doesn't make it has resale potential. Many professionals in the small business field refer to a food and drink business as a "safe business."

In a recent study by a large business brokerage firm of 1,500 businesses sold, here's a breakdown of those businesses by type:

TAVERNS/BARS

Bars
Bars with Lounge
Nightclubs and Discos
Other 3%

FAST-FOOD

Sandwich Shops
Pizza/Sandwich Shops
Chicken, Ribs, etc.
Fast-Food Franchises
Ice Cream Shops
Other 8%

RESTAURANTS

Diner Restaurants (primary function is sit-down food service)
Luncheonettes, Canteens, Snack Bars, Coffee Shops
Delis
Chinese Restaurants
Italian Restaurants
Greek Restaurants
Mexican Restaurants
Other Ethnic or Nationality Oriented Restaurants
Steak Houses
Seafood Restaurants
Novelty Food Restaurants (Gourmet, Health)
Other 11%

CATERING

Catering Trucks (Food or Ice Cream)
Catering Halls or Rooms
Other 4%

CLEANERS

Coin-Op Washers and/or Cleaning Machines
Cleaning and/or Washing—Retail
Cleaning and/or Washing—Industrial
Other 6%

MARKETS

Grocery Stores and Supermarkets
Convenience Food Stores
Fruits and Produce Stores
Meat Stores
Fish and Seafood Stores
Novelty Food (Variety, Gourmet, Health, Cheese, Candy)
Other 10%

PACKAGE/LIQUOR STORES 3%

SERVICES

Financial Services (Insurance, Credit, Investment)
Hotels, Motels, Camps
Auto/Truck Repair and Service
Home Repair and Service
Office or Commercial Repair and Service
TV and Appliance Repair and Service
Personal (Counseling, Education, Child Care)
Advertising, Printing, Artwork
Travel Agencies
Hair and/or Beauty Salons
Rental Agencies
Tailors, Shoe Repair
Construction, Landscapers

Amusement and Recreation	
Transportation (Taxi, Bus, etc.)	
Other Services	12%
RETAIL	
Fabric Stores	
Clothing and/or Shoe Stores for Men and Women	
Clothing and/or Shoe Stores for Men	
Clothing and/or Shoe Stores for Women	
Department Stores	
Photo Shops	
Gift Shops, Hobby or Craft Shops, Stationery Stores	
Auto/Truck Parts/Tire Stores	
Auto/Truck Sales	
Pharmacies, Opticians	
Sports Stores (Bait, Tackle, Guns, Athletic Equipment)	
Furniture, TV, Appliance Stores	
Florists, Garden Centers, Nurseries	
Pet Shops	
Hardware and/or Electrical Stores	
Jewelry and/or Accessory Stores	
Audio, Video, Record and Tape Stores	
Other	15%
BAKERIES	
Retail Bakeries	
Wholesale Bakeries	
Doughnut Shops	
Novelty Bakery Shops (Bagels, etc.)	
Other	8%
OTHER	
Manufacturing	
Distribution	
Newspapers and/or Magazines	
Delivery Services	
Other	20%
	100%

The major categories of food and drink businesses from the list amount to almost one-half of the total:

Taverns/Bars	3%
Fast-Food	8%
Restaurants	11%
Catering	4%
Markets	10%
Package/Liquor Stores	3%
Bakeries	8%
Total	47%

If you want to get into business with as little downside risk as possible, food and drink is the answer.

However, because not everyone wants a food and drink related business, let's look at some other fields.

RETAIL BUSINESSES

If you know nothing about the retail apparel business such as men's and women's clothing, stay away from it. There's not much demand for closed clothing stores, and without some experience, you may be in over your head. If you have experience and knowledge in the clothing field, a lot of money has been made in jeans shops. However, like most retail businesses, they involve a large inventory, and this inventory can create a financial stumbling block in the purchase of a retail operation.

Let's talk about some other retail possibilities. Keep in mind that all successful retail businesses have one thing in common: the people who run them enjoy people, all kinds of people. Even nasty, demanding customers are seen as challenges, not irritants. If you're secure in your feelings about your ability to deal positively with people, then you can successfully run many retail businesses with little background or experience. Card and gift shops fall easily into this category. We know of a small lamp shop in suburban Boston whose large selection makes it fun to browse through. The owners concentrate on personalized service. You'd never guess they didn't know anything about lamps when they bought the business. The wine and cheese store several doors down is owned and operated by a former schoolteacher and his family. When he bought the store five years ago, the only thing he knew about wine and cheese was how to drink and eat it; now he's a recognized expert in both fields. The toy store across from the lamp shop is owned by two women whose husbands are quite successful in their own right. These delightful ladies don't operate the business just for money, although it is profitable. These owners of one of the most quaint, delightful toy stores you could find had no background in toys other than years of buying them for their own children.

If you're mechanically inclined, an auto parts business may interest you. However, the large inventory usually maintained by such businesses can add considerably to the purchase price. Remember, many sellers want cash for their inventory when they sell. A $30,000 inventory in some businesses is not uncommon, and if you have to come up with a down payment plus buy the inventory, you could be spending $50,000 in no time.

Stationery stores, flower shops, hobby shops, pet shops, arts and crafts centers—the list goes on and on—all offer real possibilities. Although product knowledge is helpful and probably necessary, it can be acquired. The real key is your ability to deal with people. How many times have you been in a department store where the salespeople look the other way when you need help, or even ignore you when you have an item and want to pay for it? Whether you experience this from the owner or an employee, the result is the same: you probably won't go back. If your ability to work with people doesn't permit you to serve customers cheerfully, or to effectively select, train, and manage employees to do this for you, forget about buying a retail business. You'll never be happy and your chances of success will be greatly reduced.

SERVICE BUSINESSES

Service businesses aren't as easy to define as retail ones. Consultants, cosmetologists, lawyers, travel and employment agents, physicians, and counselors all represent service businesses. What elements are involved in the successful purchase or ownership of such a business?

The purchase of a service business usually does not require as large an investment in equipment or inventory as retail, manufacturing, or wholesaling businesses. Obviously, beauty and barber shops have equipment, but if it is not brand new, the cost won't be exorbitant and it can often be financed.

Some service businesses require licenses to operate, and in some cases there are minimum educational, experience, and testing requirements to be fulfilled before a license can be obtained. Legal and medical practitioners, and individuals selling real estate or insurance are in this category. You may be able to own such businesses or have an investment in one, but you can't work if you aren't licensed.

Service businesses may also require specialized knowledge. For example, although state licensing is not required in most areas, full service travel agencies must employ experienced travel agents to compete successfully. We all probably feel we could operate an ice cream store, but how many of us are ready to get into a financial service business where we manage other people's money? You can't usually enter that business without experience and succeed. Advertising and public relations businesses pose similar problems.

How important is experience in a service business? Although the hotel and motel industry offers many opportunities, if you're going to buy a Hyatt Regency Hotel, you'd better get some prior experience. On the other hand, many smaller motels are operated quite nicely by competent but previously inexperienced people.

Many service businesses such as travel agencies have been purchased by inexperienced people, but they retain (under an employment contract) the previous owner or an experienced employee to manage the business for them.

What should you avoid in considering the purchase of service businesses? Remember, as a first-timer, time isn't always on your side. Stay away from trendy or faddish businesses. Remember skateboard parks and trampoline centers? They sprang up everywhere and died just as quickly. Not long ago, tanning centers were the thing; now there aren't many left. Video and arcade game centers are now very popular, and video games are found in other businesses such as convenience food stores, motels and hotels, airports, and pizza parlors. Everybody's in the act, but community government is fighting them every step of the way, and the public may soon tire of this form of amusement.

Although cleaning operations are considered a separate category of small business, they're really service businesses. Dry cleaning and coin-operated laundries are relatively safe to purchase; they're easy to run and can be very profitable. George Naddaff, Chairman of VR Business Brokers, Inc., and an entrepreneur's entrepreneur, feels dry cleaning is a boom business. He's particularly excited about all the possibilities for expanded services that can be offered from a dry cleaning facility: shoe repair, key duplication, film development, tailoring, monogramming, rug cleaner rental.

Coin-operated laundries can be profitable, but you almost always need more than one to make a living. People with four or five coin-operated laundries usually do quite well, but don't get into this business unless you or someone in your family is quite handy.

Service businesses are the most rapidly growing segment of the economy. If you have specific training or skills, look into offering those to others through the purchase of a service business. The major advantages of buying a service business are: it usually doesn't take a lot of money, it has less down-side risk because there's little inventory or equipment involved, and space requirements are minimal.

OTHER BUSINESSES

In our previous discussion we talked about food and drink businesses, which make up 47 percent of the sample of the 1,500 operations, other retail businesses (15 percent) and service businesses (18 percent). This leaves us with the remaining 20 percent made up primarily of manufacturing and distribution businesses.

A distribution business (a beer distributor, for example) works on a low profit margin and therefore must often move large inventories in order to be profitable and provide the owner with a reasonable salary. If large inventories are necessary, a significant investment in warehousing must be made, and there goes the price.

Distribution businesses are simple to operate, though. They are suppliers of goods to the business (the beer companies in the case of our beer distributor) and there are established customers (stores, bars, restaurants). It's just a matter of keeping the proper balance between the two. Many people want distribution or wholesaling operations because of their simplicity, but because the price may include real estate as well as inventory, it's generally beyond the range of the small business investment we're talking about here.

Small manufacturing businesses abound, but you must remember, these are the most complex businesses to operate. You must purchase the proper types of raw materials, convert them to a finished product, find customers for that product, and sell it to them at a profit. Compare that to a retail operation, where the only conversion necessary is taking a completed product out of a carton, sticking it on the shelf, and then selling it to the customer who walks in the door.

Don't buy a manufacturing company unless you have manufacturing experience.

BUSINESS AND SKILLS ASSESSMENT

Let's look at some areas that will enable you to think about your own desires and skills as a prospective business owner. The first checklist gives you an opportunity to set down some of the beginning criteria for the business you are seeking. If you're unclear about some of these items, leave them blank for now, but keep in mind they should be settled in the future. The second list enables you to assess the skills that are important in running a successful business. If you find there are large gaps in your business skills in these areas, you may need to gain more knowledge and experience before buying a business.

BUSINESS CRITERIA

1. Where will this business be located (town, state)?

2a. When will I begin looking for the business (month, year)? [NOTE: Even if you are highly unsure of your timing, estimate this as closely as possible.]

b. When will I begin operating the business?

3. My business must eventually have the following characteristics; [NOTE: These could be measurable quantities like sales of $500,000 or intangible items like quality.]

   a.
   b.
   c.
   d.
   e.

4. My business must *not* have the following characteristics:

   a.
   b.
   c.
   d.
   e.

5. Here is a list of businesses (restaurant, office service firm, mail order) that appeal to me:

   a.
   b.
   c.
   d.
   e.

6. Here is a list of businesses that do not appeal to me:

   a.
   b.
   c.
   e.

7. My lifestyle demands that I earn the following annual salary:

   $________

8. I eventually want to work ________ hours per week:

   ☐ less than 20
   ☐ 20 to 40
   ☐ 40 to 60
   ☐ 60 to 80
   ☐ more than 80

9. Which of the following best applies to me? (More than one could apply):

   ☐ I want to buy a small business and keep the business small.
   ☐ I want the business to grow to a moderate size.
   ☐ I want to buy a business that could grow quite large.

☐ I will probably run the business for the rest of my life.

☐ I will build the business, sell it, and start another.

☐ I will build the business, sell it, and retire or do something else.

☐ Other. Specify:

10. What customer group do I want to serve?

☐ The consumer (the general public)

☐ Other businesses or industry

☐ Professional organizations (accountants, lawyers)

☐ Non-profit organizations (YMCAs, churches)

☐ Special groups (farmers, pilots). Specify:

☐ State or local government

☐ Federal government

☐ Foreign (export)

☐ Other. Specify:

11. What kind of a business will this be?

☐ Retail

☐ Wholesale

☐ Service

☐ Transportation

☐ Construction

☐ Manufacturing

☐ Other. Specify:

12. Will there be others buying this business with me?

☐ No

☐ Yes

If yes, list person(s) and relationship (friend, spouse) if any:

	Name	*Relationship*
a.		
b.		
c.		

13. Who will be my advisors?

	Name	*Address*
a. Attorney		
b. Accountant		
c. Insurance Agent		
d. Consultant		
e. Other		

14. How do I want to sell my products or services?

☐ Myself

☐ Employed salespeople

☐ Sales representatives (non-employees)

☐ Distributors/dealers

☐ Mail

☐ Other. Specify:

15. List below any assured income from trusts, real estate investments, and the like:

	Source	*Estimated Annual Income*
a.		
b.		
c.		

16. Make a list below of any relatives or friends who might be approached for money later on:

	Name	*Relationship*
a.		
b.		
c.		
d.		
e.		

17. What are my important reasons for wanting to go into my own business? [NOTE: More than one may apply.]

☐ Believe I can "do it better" than existing competition.

☐ It's a dream. (No negative intent.)

☐ Don't like where I live now.

☐ Can't work for someone else.

☐ Want to make a lot of money.

☐ Want independence.

☐ Quit my job.

☐ Was fired.

☐ Fed up with corporate life.

☐ Want legacy for my children.

☐ Need tax shelter.

☐ Want to prove myself.

☐ Can't get along with bosses.

☐ Have unused talents.

☐ Want to do it my way without compromise.

☐ Want to be of real service to others.

☐ Family can work together.

☐ Other. Specify:

18. What are my major reservations about being in business?

☐ Fear of failure.

☐ Lack of business knowledge.

☐ Too much work.

☐ Giving up present pay and benefits.

☐ Leaving/losing present friends, if moving.

- ☐ No time for family.
- ☐ Giving up present outside activities.
- ☐ Might get locked in.
- ☐ Lack of confidence.
- ☐ Not enough money of my own.
- ☐ Not knowing where to turn for help.
- ☐ Acting impulsively.
- ☐ Acting too slowly.
- ☐ Fear of success.
- ☐ The entire question of risk.
- ☐ Fear of change.
- ☐ Discomfort with ill-defined situation—the unknown.
- ☐ Other. Specify:

SKILLS CHECKLIST

I believe I have sufficient knowledge and background to buy and run my own business.

Business Skill	YES	NO	UNCERTAIN
I. SALES AND MARKETING			
A. Marketing Research—Discovering market conditions and analyzing customer demand.			
B. Marketing Planning—Using marketing information for planning.			
C. Pricing—Setting final prices that will be profitable but not out of reach of the customer.			
D. Advertising/Public Relations—Using both message and media in a proper balance to increase customer demand and awareness.			
E. Sales Management—Supervising others in the selling process.			
F. Personal Selling—Am I or can I be an effective salesperson?			
G. Sales Administration—Knowledge of marketing law.			
H. Competitive Analysis—Keeping abreast of what my competition is doing.			
II. BUSINESS OPERATION			
A. Purchasing—How to buy goods and services at minimum prices and best terms.			
B. Inventory Control—How to keep supplies and raw materials at levels that are neither too high nor too low.			
C. Scheduling—When to make certain events in a business occur for maximum effectiveness: a sense of timing.			
D. Quality Control—How much effort to expend towards assuring proper quality consistent with price and customer expectation.			
E. Business Planning—How to prepare and follow a business plan.			
F. Expansion—How to plan for and use growth without running out of control.			
III. FINANCE			
A. Bookkeeping—The recording of accounting information in journals and ledgers.			

SKILLS CHECKLIST

Business Skill	YES	NO	UNCERTAIN
B. Accounting—Understanding the key financial statements of a business, the income statement, and the balance sheet.			
C. Budgeting—Doing a cash flow projection and using deviations to analyze estimated vs. actual performance.			
D. Cost Control—Not only being able to detect excess expenses but doing something about it.			
E. Credit and Collection—Knowing the proper circumstances in which to extend or deny credit and being able to collect overdue accounts.			
F. Raising Money—Ability to deal with banks and other financial sources to secure capital.			
G. Banking Relations—Knowing what banks expect from a small business.			
H. Breakeven Analysis—Knowing how to do it, what it means.			
I. Ratio Analysis—Using financial ratios to further assess information on the income statement and balance sheet.			
J. Taxes—A basic understanding of the difference between personal and business taxes.			
IV. ADMINISTRATION			
A. Team Building—Selecting team members, hiring, firing, training, motivating, and leadership.			
B. Personnel Policies—Pay and benefits, labor guidelines, tax withholding, payroll reports (federal and state).			
C. Dealing with Professionals—accountants, attorneys, consultants, the SBA.			
D. Using Information—Where to get information and how to put it to proper use.			
E. Technology—The use of devices such as small business computers and word processors.			
F. Business Laws—A basic understanding of what is legal and illegal.			
TOTALS			

NOTE: There are 30 items in the skills checklist. You should have a *minimum* of 15 in the YES column.

If you have been completing the exercises in this book, go back now and review what you've learned. In Chapter One you completed a brief entrepreneurial assessment and gave yourself a letter grade. If that grade was a "D" or an "F," examine the categories in which you did not answer "yes" or "agree." Next, make a list of those items or characteristics where you fall short and ask yourself what barriers and beliefs stand in the way of your making the needed changes. The second exercise, the one on business criteria in this chapter, may have many entries that you left blank. If this is the case, you may be unclear about what you really want. Remember, the more definitive you can be, the greater the probability you will find what you want. The skills checklist tells you where you are weak. Pay close attention to the four categories of business skills—sales and marketing, business operation, finance, and administration.

See if any of those categories have a majority of "no" or "uncertain" answers. If so, you may need more learning or experience. For example, if your knowledge of finance is weak, take a two-semester course in accounting, read books, or attend seminars on the subject.

Thinking about yourself, your environment, your skills and your desires in relation to the kind of business you want are important preliminary steps to make *before* you contact a business broker or respond to a newspaper ad. Buying a business is a major step because you're really buying an entire way of life, and it may represent the largest single financial commitment you ever make. The more information you have about yourself and your desires, the better the chance you'll find what you want and be happy and successful at it.

Chapter THREE

Discovering Opportunities

PREPARATORY CONSIDERATIONS

There are undoubtedly many things that could come under the heading of preparatory considerations, but the major ones are where you're going to live, your job, and your family. Let's briefly cover these areas before we start talking about your quest for your dream business.

We've already discussed the different kinds of locale—rural, urban, suburban. If you plan to pick up roots and go somewhere else, be sure to consider the following:

1. There are tax implications connected with looking for a business in a different locale. Some of the expenses incurred looking for a business may be deductible. If you sell your house and don't purchase a new one, you may pay a hefty capital gains tax. Discuss these possibilities with your accountant or tax preparer because the laws may change from year to year.
2. If you leave a residence, whether you own it or not, you may want to find a business which includes a residence, such as an inn, motel, or even a store with owner quarters.

A former sales manager for a national manufacturer of pumps bought an old inn in need of repairs. After he turned the inn around from a losing business to a profitable one, he drew only $6,000 a year for his own personal use. Why so little? For one thing, he lived at the inn and ate most of his meals there; for another his car belonged to the corporation. Essentially his needs for lodging and transportation were taken care of, and he enjoyed legal tax benefits not available to those who aren't self-employed.

If you're presently employed and plan to quit prior to moving, plan the separation so it occurs on your terms and with proper timing. If you get yourself fired, then your plans must change accordingly. Some folks consider getting themselves laid off so that they can collect unemployment while looking for a business. In addition to being morally questionable, this may also raise some legal questions. To receive unemployment payments in most states you must

1. lose your job through no fault of your own,
   and
2. be available for and willing to work in your field.

If you plan to look for your own business, you certainly cannot satisfy the second requirement.

If you leave a job, don't overlook any payments due you from your employer: accrued vacation or sick pay, pension benefits, profit sharing. Also, see if you can continue your medical insurance on your own if your employer provides this benefit.

Finally, one strong warning regarding your present job: even if you hate and distrust your employer, fight the urge to burn that bridge. It won't accomplish anything and may harm you later on.

The third preparatory step concerns your family: spouse and children. If you plan to work with your spouse in the business, be very certain the two of you will enjoy "bumping into each other behind the cash register," as one couple put it.* Some characteristics of a successful business team are:

1. Willingness to identify as a *we.*
2. Open, honest communications.
3. Ability to keep business conflicts out of the marital relationship.
4. Strong self-esteem in each partner.
5. Ability to function independently, but willingness to confer on important matters.
6. Adaptability.

Talk with other couples who run their own businesses. Not every husband–wife team can be together all day, every day.

We're often asked about business ownership as a cause of divorce. Does self-employment contribute to the eventual separation of a man and woman? Here's our rule:

> If the marriage bond is strong, owning and running a business will only strengthen it. If the bond is weak, the added responsibility will contribute to its further deterioration.

* It might be a good idea to read Chapter 12, "Husbands and Wives As Entrepreneurs" in *How To Prosper In Your Own Business* by Brian R. Smith (The Lewis Publishing Co., 1983).

WHERE TO BEGIN LOOKING

Every business is for sale; always begin with that assumption to discover business opportunities. Most folks who are new to the game look over ads in the newspapers or contact a business broker. We'll discuss those approaches, but we also want to mention some others. Keep in mind that you are about to make a major step in your life and the process shouldn't be rushed, especially the first time around. Your search must be well planned if you are to succeed. Depending on your skill and your finances, your search may take several weeks or even a year or more to do it right. If you try to rush the process, you may

- get into a business you don't enjoy
- pay too much
- buy a business with a fatal flaw.

There are too many good businesses for sale or potentially for sale for you to settle for something far removed from what you want.

Let's start our discussion by turning the tables.

BUYER INITIATIVE

You may want to consider contacting business owners on your own behalf to determine if they would consider selling. This can be done in person, by phone, by mail, or by advertising as a potential buyer.

If you do it in person or by phone, be sure to say who you are and what you're looking for. Business owners, especially those with successful businesses, are used to receiving regular inquiries, often from brokers. Be honest and open. Don't be discouraged if a few people hang up or ask you to leave. Always handle the in-person approach with extreme care. For example, an owner who may be interested in selling may not want to begin any conversation about the subject with employees around.

If the owner agrees to a meeting following your phone conversation, don't begin by asking a lot of questions about annual sales, profits, or possible selling price. Similarly, don't volunteer information about how much you're willing to spend. Consider that first face-to-face meeting as a fishing expedition for both you and the owner. Its purpose is simply to get to know one another, to see if the two of you should go further in your mutual investigation. It is *not* the time to analyze the business or begin price and terms negotiations, so be very cautious towards owners who push the sale. That may very well be a sign of a distressed business. In your first go-around in business ownership, avoid buying a failing operation with hopes of turning it around. That takes a real pro, someone with considerable experience.

Another buyer approach is the direct mail campaign. When Celeste Redford wanted to buy a small gift store, she chose a mailing company to help her identify the prospective seller. From a list in the Yellow Pages under "Mailing Lists," she chose a company that segments businesses by location (choosing appropriate ZIP codes), by type (using the government's Standard Industrial Classification, or SIC code), and by size (annual sales). The company also does the mailing itself, producing individualized letters addressed to the business owner. Celeste's letter looked like this:

Dear Mr. Jones:

I am interested in buying a small gift store doing less than $200,000 in annual sales. I am not a broker, but am acting in my own behalf.

If you would consider the possible sale of your business, please contact me by mail or phone. Naturally, I will treat all discussions we might have in confidence.

Sincerely yours,
Celeste T. Redford
Telephone:
(216) 485-2271

If you use the mail approach, don't use a phony name or only a box number; that only lessens the number of responses. Also, don't mount a big mail campaign during a busy season such as Christmas.

What kind of response can you expect from a mail campaign? That's hard to say, but you can safely count on a 5 percent return—five responses to every 100 letters. Four businesses out of those five will probably be unsuitable for one reason or another—size, profitability, location, problems with the owner.

One other technique is to place an ad in a local paper stating you're looking for a business. When using this approach

1. Be as specific as possible about the type of business (women's clothing store, restaurant), location (within 25 miles of Oklahoma City), and size (under $250,000 annual sales).
2. Run the ad more than once—for example, once a week for three weeks.
3. State you are a principal, not a broker.
4. Decide whether or not to use a blind approach. All newspapers provide their box numbers for ad responses for a small fee; this enables you to remain anonymous. If you want to be contacted directly, give your address or your phone number or both in the ad.

Here's a sample ad:

> **QUALIFIED BUYER** looking for a hardware store or small home center in greater Des Moines. Phone principal at (515) 672-5785.

Remember, you're bound to receive a fair number of responses that are inappropriate.

ASKING AROUND

Some potential business owners mount a word-of-mouth campaign to discover possible buyers. If you have a good relationship with a commercial banking officer, he or she may know of businesses that might be for sale. Accountants, business consultants, lawyers, and the local chamber of commerce may also have some leads.

A variation of this approach is to contact people who call on the kinds of businesses you're interested in. Let's say you're looking for a grocery store. Speak to suppliers who make regular deliveries to these stores. Tell them what you're looking for and offer a finder's fee to anyone who gives you a lead that eventually leads to a business purchase.

HOW TO READ A SELLER'S AD

Many folks in the business world believe that all businesses advertised for sale in newspapers (or trade journals) are dogs. That simply isn't so. Admittedly some are losers but not all of them. For sellers who choose not to use brokers, ads are often the normal course for them to use.

Usually ads don't tell you much. Consider the following:

> **CLOTHING STORE**
>
> Full line. High sales and profit. Good location. Reasonable price and terms. Write Box 72.

It says nothing about

1. What the business actually sells. A "full line" could be women's lingerie or children's clothes.
2. The actual sales and profit. "High" means many things to many people.
3. Where the business is located—out in the sticks, in a shopping center, downtown.
4. The price.
5. Whether you're responding directly to the owner or not.

Now let's look at some business ads with specifics added:

> **MEN'S CLOTHING STORE**
>
> Full line of men's suits, coats, and casual wear. Annual sales $300,000. Profitable. Located in major shopping center. Asking price of $100,000 includes inventory. Some seller financing available. Call owner at 397-2701 evenings.

This tells you a lot more.

This doesn't mean you absolutely should not respond to vague ads. After all, a first-time business owner may be just as inexperienced at selling a business as you are in buying one. If you do answer one of these limited information ads, ask for a minimum of three things: location, annual sales, and asking price, assuming the ad at least tells you what kind of business is for sale. If that's unclear, ask for that information also.

Don't forget: you're only gathering information—finding out what's for sale, maybe making some visits. Negotiations with the seller, analysis of the business, and determination of price and terms come later.

Some prospective buyers read newspaper ads for several weeks before making any inquiry at all. One fellow we know saw the same business go from an asking price of $200,000 to $125,000 in a period of six weeks.

It almost goes without saying that you should be cautious about come-ons like: "chance of a lifetime," "no money down," "price negotiable," "Brand new equipment." This kind of hype usually spells a problem of one kind or another. For instance, "new equipment" may mean the business didn't last long enough for anything to be used, or the equipment purchased was inappropriate.

However, if you see an ad that interests you, don't hesitate to call. Take into account the kind of business you're calling so you phone at the most advantageous time. You don't call a coffee shop at lunch time; you don't call a toy store on the last shopping day before Christmas and expect a lot of information. A typical call might go as follows:

SELLER: "Hello, Joe's Deli."
YOU: "My name is Robert Dickson and I'm calling about your ad in the *Logan Gazette.* Could you answer a few questions for me now?" (You want to make sure the seller is free to answer your questions thoroughly. If he's busy, arrange a time to call back.)
SELLER: "Sure, what do you want to know?"
YOU: "How much are you asking for your business?"
SELLER: "$75,000; it's a darn good business."
YOU: "How long have you owned it?"
SELLER: "Ten years."
YOU: "Why are you selling?"
SELLER: "My wife and I want to retire and move to Florida."
YOU: "What kind of terms are you offering? (Take your ear away from the phone, just in case.)
SELLER: "What do you mean terms? I have to have it all in cash. What do you think I am—a bank? $75,000 cash and it's a steal at that price." (You might as well get used to it. Many sellers think their business is worth a fortune. Let them have their say. Don't be upset by his "all cash" statement. When the time comes, he may take terms and reduce his price too.)
YOU: "I was just inquiring. Could you tell me what the business nets?"
SELLER: "If you're interested, come on down and talk."
YOU: "That's a good idea. Where are you located?"
SELLER: "444 Main Street—next to the bank."
YOU: "Yes, I know where you are. What's the best time?"
SELLER: "It's usually quiet between 2:00 P.M. and 4:00 P.M."

If the business sounds good or intriguing, make an appointment. A lot depends on just how much time you really have. If the deli sounds just okay—tell him you'll get back to him. Perhaps you are just not ready. However, if you are serious and the deli is something you're really interested in, or think you are—go see Joe. You don't *have* to buy!

THE ISSUE OF BROKERS

Once you find a few businesses for sale by owners, you're on your way. Now it's time to visit at least two business brokers—three would be better. If you're still working, take a day or two of vacation time for this if you have to. This is important, especially if the pressures are mounting. Just like finding a job or looking for a house—this is serious business. By visiting sellers first you'll be more aware of the process and consequently more at ease when you meet your first broker.

In general there are three kinds of brokers:

1. Professionals from a field other than brokerage, such as attorneys or accountants.
2. Real estate agents.
3. Business brokers.

We do not recommend using the first two. Attorneys often become involved in the sale of a business when the business is one step away from being declared bankrupt. The same also holds true when banks are involved in the sale. Real estate agents may be fine when it comes to buying or selling a residence, but few understand business and may consciously or unconsciously mislead you.

If you use a broker, by all means use a qualified business broker. Brokers may work independently as part of large real estate offices, or members of firms specializing in the sale of small businesses. Many advertise in newspapers; others are listed in the Yellow Pages under "Business Brokers."

A broker shouldn't represent both the buyer and the seller. Normally they represent the seller, but it is possible to have a business broker represent you. In that case the broker conducts a mail and phone search for the business you specify. Generally you pay a fee for this service, which is deducted from the broker's sales commission if you buy a business through him or her.

HOW TO DEAL WITH BUSINESS BROKERS

Most active business brokers receive from 100 to 200 telephone calls per month from people just like you who call in response to their ads.

Honest brokers advertise actual businesses they have for sale, but the purpose of the ad is to get you to call—not to buy that particular business. Less than 20 percent of the people who call a broker buy the business advertised. Once you identify the ad as being a broker's, there's no point in circling any more ads belonging to that broker because a good broker will show you all the businesses that may interest you if he believes you're a qualified buyer.

Business brokers can be of great assistance, but remember, they also work on a straight commission. No sale—no paycheck. The seller pays the broker anywhere from 6 percent to 12 percent of the full purchase price. Most brokers also have a minimum charge. For example, if their commission is 10 percent of the sale price and a business sells for $35,000, they may not feel a $3,500 commission is adequate to cover their expenses. They may set a minimum commission of, for example, $5,000. Then, regardless of the selling price, if it's under $50,000, the commission rate is $5,000. If the business sells for $50,000 or more, the 10 percent rate applies. This is the total commission a brokerage office earns, which is divided among the sales person or broker who obtained the listing or found the business, the broker who sells the business, and the office itself.

You may want to see more than one broker for several reasons:

- Many brokers don't exchange business listings, so you have to go to each one to find out what's available.
- Just as with any professional, such as an attorney, accountant or banker, you need to talk to several to see if you can get along with them. You can't take full advantage of someone's knowledge and experience if you don't like him or her.

What happens during that first visit to a broker? If the broker's doing his job correctly, he'll spend the first few minutes finding out about you: what kind of work you do, your family, your interests. He'll try to find some common ground to help you relax, to gain your confidence. In order to sell you a business, he has to know something about you and your business interests.

When he feels the time is right, he'll ask about your finances. He needs to know the amount of money you're willing to put as a down payment toward the purchase of a business. The broker is not being nosy; he needs to know. If he's properly trained and knows his inventory of businesses for sale, he has a feel for what kind of down payment the sellers might consider. There's no reason for the broker to show you businesses you can't afford.

The broker may ask some penetrating questions about money you have and where that money is. Is it in a bank or other place where you can get it easily? Are you going to borrow it against your house, and if so, have you applied for the loan yet? If you're inheriting the money from old Uncle Charlie, how sick is he? If he's 45, it may be a long wait for the inheritance. The broker needs to know if you have the financial means to buy a business now.

After the broker determines how much money you can spend on the down payment and where it is, he'll want to know *when* you want to buy a business. If you're 60 years old and looking for a business to buy when you retire at 65, the broker will be polite and informative, but he'll put you in the same category as those with no money. If you have the money and are recently unemployed—look out; you have found an instant friend. Once the broker knows you have money, it's in the bank and you just left your job, the next thing he has to find out is if you're the decision maker. You may meet all the requirements to qualify as a willing buyer, but if your spouse participates in all decisions, the broker needs his or her involvement also. If you plan to go into business with a partner, you should go to the broker's office together so the broker doesn't have to go through the whole thing twice.

There's one other area the well-trained broker will explore. He'll try to find out if you have what are called "unrealistic expectations." Are you looking for a Cadillac at a Chevrolet price? This can be a very tough thing for a broker to determine. All of us want to get as much as possible for our money, but how realistic is it to want to buy a $150,000 business that nets $25,000 a year for a dollar down? It's O.K. to want that, but if the broker thinks your requirements are impractical or unattainable, he'll be much less likely to take you to look at businesses. If he takes you to see a business and tells you it's one of the best he has available, and you think it's a dump, it's time to re-evaluate your relationship with the broker and your expectations. Be honest with the broker and request the same from him or her. Say the place looks like a dump and then restate the kind of business you want. Sometimes brokers simply don't understand the buyer's needs and merely restating them puts you on the right track. Other times it's a question of the buyers' expectations far exceeding their budgets. Showing a more realistic business within the buyer's range is the way some brokers attempt to handle this problem indirectly. Rather than showing you a Cadillac and saying you can't afford it, they show you the Chevrolet you can. If you're confused or disappointed, say so. Potential buyers can have unrealistic expectations for a business. They may also have them for brokers, and brokers themselves are not immune from this phenomenon.

What can brokers do for you? Brokers usually have quite a few businesses for sale and they can help you sort out the ones that might meet your requirements. Brokers are also good sources of other information. Good brokers know about the problems associated with a business purchase, and they know the technical aspects of business licensing, tax implications, utility transfers and everything else you need to do to put the business in proper operating order. A good broker handles all seller negotiations, makes sure the lease problems are resolved, and manages all the legal details of the business transfer. A good broker also educates you in the business buying process. Most of what you're told will be honest, straightforward advice, but remember, it's also self-serving.

After the educational period, the broker arranges for you to see some businesses. He selects suitable prospects for your inspection based on your responses to his questions. Does it have to be a doughnut shop? How much income do you need? Does the business have to be in a specific part of town? Is your family going to work with you? Can you get more money if you need it? If you're interested in a business that is involved in alcoholic beverages, such as a tavern or a liquor store, is there any reason, such as prior illegal activity, that would prevent you getting a liquor license from the state? A good broker knows his inventory of businesses for sale, those 10 to 15 he likes the most, knows the best, and feels are the most saleable he currently has available. Based on what he knows about you, he chooses the businesses you will see. If he knows you're an amateur photographer, he may show you a camera shop. If he discovers you're a tropical fish enthusiast, he may have a tropical fish-store for you to take a look at. That doughnut shop in the ad that originally brought you to the broker may not even show up at all. Even though the broker may show you businesses you really haven't given much thought to, let him go through his inventory. You may get some pleasant surprises.

HOW BROKERS WORK

Sellers contact brokers or vice versa. If the broker feels the business is saleable, and the seller agrees to work with the broker and pay the broker's commission, they execute a listing agreement. There are two basic kinds of agreements:

1. The exclusive right to sell. In this case the seller pays the broker's commission regardless of who sells the business, including the seller.
2. The exclusive agency. Here the broker is the only outsider (agent) who can sell the business and earn a commission. The seller can act on his or her own.

There is also an open listing but it's rarely used in the sale of businesses.

On the next page is a standard listing agreement for an exclusive right to sell. It represents the minimum

LISTING AGREEMENT

Date ___/___/___

Type of Business ________________
Address ________________
City ________________
Phone No. ________________
Corp. &/or Firm Name ________________
dba ________________
Seller's Name ________________
Address ________________
City ________________
Phone No. ________________
Bldg. Size ________ Seats ________
No. Employees ________ F.T. ________ P.T.
Payroll $________ Per Month ________
License Required? ________________
Parking ________________
Days Open ________ Closed On ________
Hours Open ________________

Base Mo. Rental ________ Lease Exp. Date ________
Option ________ Years Security on Lease $________
Terms and Conditions ________________
Misc. Lease Information ________________
Landlord ________ Phone ____/____
Property Mgr. ________ Phone ____/____
Estab. ________ Yrs. Pres. Owner ________ Yrs.
Furn., Equip. $________ incl. in purch. price
Inventory at Cost $________ incl. in purch. price
Monthly Receipts $________, Seller will prove
Monthly Net Profit $________, Seller will prove
Purchase Price $________ Includes $________ Comm.
Down Payment $________ Includes $________ Comm.
Seller will carry balance at $________ per month inc.
________ % interest on unpaid balance
Additional Terms ________________

REASON FOR SALE ________________

LIENS/ENCUMBRANCES Total $________

Amount $________ Payments $________ Interest ____ % Holder ________ Phone ____/____
Amount $________ Payments $________ Interest ____ % Holder ________ Phone ____/____

All trade fixtures and equipment included except the following items: ________________

REMARKS

SOLE AND EXCLUSIVE RIGHT TO SELL

1. The Seller hereby engages the Broker, on a sole and exclusive basis, to sell the above described property, including all fixtures, goodwill, trademarks, trade names and inventory associated therewith.

2. Seller agrees to pay Broker ________ (%), but in any event not less than $________, of the purchase price.

3. Seller agrees that if this listing is cancelled or the property withdrawn from sale during the listing term by Seller, the commission shall become immediately due by Seller to Broker. If Seller refuses or is unable to comply with the listing terms for any reason, thereby preventing disposition of the property during the listing term upon the terms set forth above, the commission shall become immediately due by the Seller to the Broker.

4. Seller agrees that the commission shall be immediately due and payable if the Seller, directly or indirectly, enters into a Purchase and Sale Agreement (however designated) accepts a deposit or does any other act tantamount to a sale or contract to sell without the written approval of the Broker, and the cancellation or recission of any of the foregoing acts shall not act as a release of Seller for such liability.

5. In any case where the deposit and/or down payment have been forfeited, the deposit shall be split 50% to Seller and 50% to Broker.

6. The Seller acknowledges that s/he has supplied the listing information above and Seller warrants such information to be true and correct.

7. Seller agrees to pay the full commission set forth in this Agreement to the Broker in the event the property described herein is, within one year after the termination of this Agreement, sold, traded or otherwise conveyed to anyone referred to Seller by the Broker or with whom Seller had negotiations during the term of this Agreement.

8. This Agreement shall commence on the day and year set forth below and continue until   , 19   .

9. Should any suit be commenced to enforce the Broker's rights herein, in the event the Broker is successful the Seller agrees to pay the Broker the expenses connected therewith, including attorney's fees incurred.

10. Seller hereby acknowledges that s/he has read this agreement and has received a copy of it.

11. If Seller is a partnership, corporation or other entity, the person(s) signing on behalf of such entity hereby represent(s) and warrant(s) that s/he has, or they have the authority to enter into this contract on behalf of said entity.

Employment Accepted by Broker:

OFFICE NAME ________________
OFFICE ADDRESS ________________
LISTING AGENT ________________

____
Corp. Name
____
Seller
____
Seller
DATE ________________

information given by the seller to the broker. It gives you an idea of the actual information that the broker has available, although his or her knowledge of the history of the business may be more important than the information furnished on the listing.

The real business is between the lines, and a good broker knows that information. As a potential buyer, you need the knowledge to read between the lines also. Brokers don't necessarily look at the printed facts, although they are important; they look at the unsaid. For example, what kind of guy is the seller? If there's a lease, what's the landlord like? Brokers should know or have access to the real inside information about the businesses they show you.

When a broker refers businesses to you, you will be asked to sign a form stating that the broker was the first to put you and the owner together. The purpose of this form (see below) is to protect the broker's commission. Regardless of the wording or the size of the form, the purpose is the same. It shows the broker as the procuring cause (in other words, he introduced you to the business owner) and is entitledto a commission.

Depending on the form used, if you deceive the broker and the seller, you could be responsible for the commission, even though you're the buyer. If you don't tell one broker or the seller you saw the business through the efforts of another broker, you could face some legal action for recovery of the commission. If you and the seller work together to beat the broker out of the commission, you both could be in trouble.

If you're honest, you have nothing to fear by signing this form. Play it straight and don't get caught between two brokers on the same business. The fault will be yours by allowing two brokers to work with you on the same business.

Many brokers personally take you to inspect the businesses and go through the business with you. If you're ever looked at a house with a real estate broker, the procedure is basically the same.

Whether you go out on your own or are escorted by the broker, some results are the same: You get to see what's available for sale, some idea of prices, down payments, rents, leases, earnings, and a feel for what owning your own business could be like.

BUSINESS DATA FORM

Date ___/___/___

NAME AND ADDRESS	CITY, STATE	SELLER'S NAME	RENT	PRICE	TERMS

I/We the undersigned prospective purchaser(s) hereby acknowledge having been first referred and shown the above listed businesses by broker. Receipt of a copy of this Agreement is hereby Acknowledged.

Date ________________ 19 ______

By ______________________
Broker

Signature ______________________

Print Name ______________________

Address ______________________

City, State, Zip ________________ Phone (___) ________

FRANCHISES

Buying a franchise is a special form of a business acquisition. We strongly suggest you do two things first if you're thinking about this route:

1. Go to your local library or bookstore and get at least one or two books on franchising.
2. Write to the International Franchise Assn., 7315 Wisconsin Ave., N.W., Washington, DC 20014 for their informational brochures on purchasing a franchise.

A franchise is a legal relationship between the organization (the franchisor) and the owner of the establishment (the franchisee). The franchisee has the right to use the name and products of the business (McDonald's, Midas, Lawn King) and, in return, agrees to conduct the business along certain guidelines and to meet the requirements of the franchisor—you can't paint a Howard Johnson's roof green or serve whiskey sours at a Dunkin' Donuts. The legal relationship is expressed in a contract between the two parties, spelling out the terms and conditions of the franchise agreement.

A franchise is also something else. Many people believe buying a McDonald's is the same as buying a fast-food restaurant. Yes, they buy that all right, but what they really buy is a proven *method* to supply certain food items at a profit. Deviate from that method and you invite disaster.

The franchisor agrees to let the franchisee operate as a privately owned and operated business—meaning that the franchisee hires the help, pays the bills, serves as the chief executive—with the benefit of the use of the name, trademarks, and logos of the franchisor. In many cases the franchisee agrees to buy supplies from the franchisor. This is usually to the franchisee's advantage because he or she can take advantage of the greater purchasing power of the franchisor.

The franchise agreement usually covers the following items:

1. The fee—a one-time payment made by the franchisee to acquire the franchise. It does not buy anything physical like a building or inventory.
2. Other financial commitments on the part of the franchisee.
3. Payment of royalties which are often expressed as a percent of sales, which can vary from 2 percent of sales to 20 percent.
4. Training and operation manuals provided by the franchisor.
5. Exclusive territory, which may be a town, a county, or a radius of so many miles.
6. Standards for operating the business, like not allowing vending machines.
7. A lot of legalese regarding things like default, escape, termination, state of applicable law.

If you are interested in a franchise that has national stature, be sure you understand what's required. If the franchise is relatively new and untried, proceed with extreme caution and do the following:

1. Visit existing franchisees. Talk frankly with them.
2. View the business as you would any purchase. Does it make sense now and for the future?
3. In areas where franchises exist, check with the chamber of commerce and Better Business Bureau to see if complaints have been lodged against existing operations.
4. Visit the franchisor's headquarters. If there isn't one, forget the deal.
5. Have your lawyer review the franchise agreement.
6. Be sure nothing is left unresolved before signing the contract.

Remember, you can also buy a franchise that has an established location, but that you will most likely deal with the franchisor as well as the existing franchisee. The sale of an operating franchise is essentially the same as the sale of any small business with the exception of the franchise agreement. About 15 percent of the small businesses sold are existing franchises.

There's one very important point about franchises which bears repeating: you will be restricted to one degree or another in terms of what you can sell, what you can charge, how you decorate and advertise. You and your employees may even be told how to dress. If you can go along with these requirements and still feel comfortable, fine. If you want to be freer to do it your own way, then franchises aren't for you.

Chapter FOUR

The First Steps

GATHERING INITIAL INFORMATION

Having completed the exercises in this book and given serious thought to your business acquisition, you now have a good idea of the kind of business you want and where it will be located. When you begin your search—whether you use a single source like a business broker or multiple sources—you have the opportunity to gather more information about specific businesses. If you work with a broker, you can expect that individual to give you the following basic data:

1. Type of business—laundromat, barber shop, hardware store.
2. Location.
3. Condensed financial data, usually sales and profits for the past two or three years.
4. The asking price and what the price includes—inventory, physical assets, real estate.
5. Down payment and degree of seller financing.
6. Reason the owner is selling the business.

If you deal directly with the seller, he or she may be reluctant to supply this information until a personal meeting has taken place, but then should willingly supply it. If not, look out; the business could have a fatal flaw.

Whatever process you use, the idea is to rule out the obvious poor choices as early as possible. When do you begin? Stop gathering information about a particular business if it doesn't excite you or is located somewhere unappealing. Don't initially rule out an otherwise acceptable business because the price or down payment seems too high. Remember, all things are negotiable and *price* has a counterpart called *terms;* that is, *how* that price will be paid. The two go hand in hand.

Let's look at the difference between price and

terms. A buyer and a seller engage in negotiations over the sale of a small business and can't agree on the conditions. The seller, thinking himself a shrewd businessman, suggests he set the price and the buyer the terms. The buyer readily agrees to this. The seller then sets the price for the business at one million dollars, far in excess of its worth. "Fine," the buyer responds. "The terms are one dollar per year for a million years."

From our story you can see that looking only at price can be misleading. Also, don't forget, it's the buyer, not the seller, who ultimately determines the price. Unlike your negative feelings about the kind of business or its location, which can be very difficult, if not impossible to alter, price and down payment are both easily changed.

Similarly, don't drum a business out of the running because of its past financial performance. Many small businesses are often deliberately run at a small profit with an occasional loss from time to time for tax purposes. Later we'll show you how to separate these from the *real* losers.

The reason for the sale shouldn't put you off unless you detect some fatal flaw in the business that can't be corrected economically. For example, there are, for some unknown reason, doomed locations. Think of that building in your town that's been a restaurant, a motorcycle shop, and a dry cleaner-laundromat combination. No matter what anyone puts in it, no one can seem to make a go of it. Another fatal flaw is the business that was the last of its type to open in an already saturated market. Any locale can only support so many businesses of any one kind—yarn shops, gift shops, gas stations. Many people start businesses without paying attention to the *amount* of competition that already exists, and they open only to discover they can't pull enough sales from their competitors. The result? They try to sell the business to an unsuspecting buyer. Don't you be that buyer.

Some other reasons given for the sale of a business are

- Owner(s) dissatisfied, burned out, bored
- Owner(s) retiring
- Illness
- Moving
- Owner(s) want a different or larger business
- Death (estate sale)
- Divorce (must sell to settle finances)
- Too many other interests
- Spouse transferred
- Family pressures
- Internal difficulties (two or more partners who can't get along)
- Owner wants to be employed, not self-employed.

All these are legitimate reasons, but there may be something else behind them. For instance, "owner retiring" certainly sounds like an acceptable reason, but suppose the owner is 32 years old, the business has an asking price of $87,000 and debts of $50,000. No one 32 is going to retire with $37,000 unless they plan to live in the woods and eat nuts and berries. Ask a few more questions about the nature of this "retirement." The category "internal difficulties" could stem from the fact that the business is not making it for one reason or another. Find out what these internal difficulties are. We will come back to this issue in Chapter Five.

This information gathering, then, becomes your first step in buying a business. You use this information to quickly eliminate the obvious dogs. Although you may begin with a list of eight to ten businesses whose characteristics interest you, we suggest you eventually narrow it to five to seven prime business candidates. From that number, zero in on one to three operations to analyze in detail. Finally, pick one business to prepare a business plan for, negotiate price and terms, secure the necessary financing, and finally, purchase. It's a simple method, and the right way to buy a small business.

Now that we've looked at the initial information you want from the seller, let's look at the kinds of information the seller can rightfully expect from you. Doesn't it make sense that many sellers will want to know if you're qualified to buy their business? Put yourself in the seller's place for a moment: you advertise your lovely business and suddenly everyone in the world comes out of the woodwork—dissatisfied corporate executives, motorcycle mechanics, and a general collection of curiosity seekers. As a seller you want to know (1) is this person really interested in my business, and (2) are they financially qualified to buy it?

Resuming your role as a prospective buyer, you know you can show your interest by asking meaningful questions about the business, its operation, and price. But how do you prove to the seller you're financially able to buy his or her business—especially if you've never taken the time to put together any personal financial information? And do you *have* to prove this to the seller? Are we suggesting you *must* hand out this information to the owner of every business you look at? No, but on the other hand, if you feel you need certain basic financial data from the seller to convince you of his or her sincerity (and perhaps even honesty) and the suitability of the business to meet your needs, doesn't the seller have the right to similar evidence of your ability to buy that business? Can you reasonably expect a seller to be totally open with you if you are not willing to be likewise? If you find you're unwilling to give this information, even though it's readily available, perhaps this isn't the business for you. Obviously there's something about the owner you don't trust; don't ignore those feelings. Keep looking.

On the other hand, if you want to share financial data with the seller but your information is only a loose collection of bank statements, dividend reports and old income tax forms, now's the time to get organized. Before you can tell a seller where you are financially, you must first know that yourself. The best way to do that is to calculate your net worth and figure out how much you need to live on. Not only will this information help you answer the seller's questions; it will help you determine your financial needs for the future.

DETERMINING YOUR FINANCES

In this section we're going to calculate your net worth and figure out what you need to live on. Both assessments are vitally important, not only when buying but also when operating your own business. Let's begin with what you're worth in dollars and cents, your net worth.

In a net worth statement you assign a monetary value to the things you own (assets), the things you owe (liabilities), then subtract the liabilities from the assets; the result is your net worth. If your liabilities are greater than your assets, your net worth is negative and you're in a *technical* state known as insolvency. You're not bankrupt—that's a *legal* state resulting from a ruling of a federal bankruptcy court.

A net worth statement, like the balance sheet of a business, shows what happens if you convert all your assets to cash and pay off all your liabilities. Ideally, you're left with a bunch of money. It's important to analyze this because, if you're like most people who buy their own business, you're going to use some or most of your assets (cash surrender value in life insurance policies, a mutual fund, part of your pension, your house pledged as collateral for a business loan at a bank) to provide capital for the down payment. Another reason for doing a net worth analysis is that you need one to apply for a bank loan and you may need to borrow some money when you buy your business. Bankers call a net worth statement of statement of financial condition.

You can use the form provided (Figure 4–1) to do your net worth statement. Notice, the net worth statement is dated; that's because it represents a snapshot of your financial condition at a specific moment in time—a frozen frame, if you will. If today is Tuesday, June 7, 1985, your finances are different from those of next Tuesday, June 14th. In the intervening week you may deposit a pay check in your checking account, increasing your net worth; or maybe your 100 shares of Greatly Diversified Industries drop five points, decreasing your net worth by $500. Note that assets are on the left and liabilities on the right of the net worth statement. This is merely convention; there's no magic to this alignment.

Let's start with the assets (left) side. When recording amounts, don't worry about getting figures to the nearest penny. If you're within $50 of the exact figure, that's good enough.

Cash on hand: This means greens in your jeans or, as grandfather used to say, cash money. Although most people don't carry a lot of money around with them, some folks keep cash hidden somewhere in piggy banks and the like. So, if you have some mad money stashed away in a coffee can or a mattress, include it.

Cash in banks: Next to real cash money, funds in banks are the next best thing. Figure your actual checking account(s) balance(s) for the day you choose to do your net worth statement. If you haven't balanced your checking account, do it now. If you have a savings account, or several, call the bank and ask them to calculate any interest due. Put any certificates of deposit in the category called Other. Again, it's important to include any accrued interest on CDs; your local banking officer or head teller can give you this information.

Money Market: In the late 1970s when interest rates reached 20 percent, many people performed disintermediation; that is, they switched funds from one source (bank savings accounts) to another, the new money market funds. If you have one of these, write in the balance as well as any accrued interest.

U.S. Government Securities: There seem to be hundreds of kinds of government securities—treasury notes, treasury bonds, Series E bonds, Series H bonds, Fannie Maes, Ginnie Maes, repos, treasury bills, and on and on. If you have any of these, put down their present values.

Net Worth Statement of______________________________

as of ______________________________ 19_____

Assets		Liabilities	
Cash on hand	$	Notes payable to banks	$
Cash in banks		Secured	
Checking		Unsecured	
Savings		Amounts payable to others	
Other		Secured	
Money market		Unsecured	
U.S. Govt. securities		Accounts due	
Marketable securities		Credit cards	
Stocks		Installment loans	
Bonds		Other	
Mutual Funds			
Other			
Receivables			
Life Insurance (CSV)		Unpaid taxes	
Real Estate		Insurance loans	
Vehicles		Mortgages	
Personal property		Other debts	
Pension benefits		TOTAL LIABILITIES	$
Business interests		NET WORTH	$
Other Assets			
TOTAL ASSETS	$	LIABILITIES AND NET WORTH	$

Figure 4-1

Marketable Securities: For stocks—both common and preferred—give the market value on the date of the net worth statement. If you own stock in a company that's not publicly traded, you'll need to determine its value. If you own restricted stock, it's better not to assign any value to it at all because it's not marketable. Bonds include such items as convertible debentures, corporate bonds, and municipal bonds. For mutual funds, use the net asset value (NAV), which you can determine by checking the *Wall Street Journal.* Under "Other," include items such as options [puts and calls], commodity contracts, foreign bonds, margin accounts. Remember, these must be *marketable.*

Receivables: If any person or business owes you money, it's a receivable. These usually consist of loans receivable and notes receivable, the latter being represented in writing.

Life Insurance (CSV): CSV stands for cash surrender value. You may need to call your insurance agent to obtain the correct figure.

Real Estate: If you own a house, some land, or have an interest in something like a real estate investment trust, determine its fair market value; that may require professional appraisal.

Vehicles: For any automobiles, motorcycles, trucks, snowmobiles, motor homes, boats, airplanes, you need to determine the current fair market value. You can probably get these figures from an installment loan officer at your local bank.

Personal Property: Be careful with items in this category. There's a tendency to throw furniture and appliances in at either their cost when you bought them or replacement cost. Unless you have a precious oriental or a valuable silver collection, value your belongings at what they'd bring at a yard sale. However, be certain to include the value of things like coin or stamp collections.

Pension Benefits: If you work for an employer, you may have vested rights in a pension plan. Check with your personnel director. Also include the value of any IRAs or Keoughs you have.

Business Interests: If you already have a small business on the side, it has value. Check with your accountant. If you value it yourself, be very, *very* conservative.

Other Assets: People usually list the value of trusts under Other Assets. Don't list what we call contingent assets; if you're named in rich Aunt Sadie's will, that has no value until her demise. Other assets include items such as tax rebates due, insurance dividends, and profit-sharing.

Add up the assets and put the results under TOTAL ASSETS. Surprised? Many people are, but before you go off on a spending spree, remember, we still have to list liabilities, which accountants call claims against the assets. Let's start with the right-hand column. As with the assets, we won't deal with *contingent* liabilities. For example, you might be a co-maker or co-guarantor on a car loan for your sister, and if she defaults and can't pay, you'll have to. Because the liability only occurs if she fails to make the payments, it doesn't belong on a net worth statement. However, make a separate list of any contingent liabilities (co-endorser of a note, a lien against an asset such as real estate) because banks ask for that information when you apply for a loan.

Notes Payable to Banks: This category doesn't include either mortgages or car loans but represents a note in writing which is either secured (that is, backed by an asset of some kind) or unsecured.

Accounts Payable to Others: This might be a loan from your brother-in-law, a credit union loan, or other personal debts.

Acccounts Due: Under the first category, *credit cards,* list all open balances on VISA, MasterCard, gasoline credit cards, Sears, Ward, etc. In the *installment loan* category, total up loans for things like cars and recreational vehicles. Do not show items that are paid-for services like telephone or cable TV.

Unpaid Taxes: List any taxes due on both income and property. Pro-rate any property taxes. For instance, if you pay real estate taxes on your home at the end of every year (you don't have a tax escrow account) and this is June, put down one-half of the estimated annual tax.

Insurance Loans: If you borrowed against your life insurance, figure in the total amount you've borrowed. Note that, if on the asset side you put down *net* CSV (total CSV less outstanding loans), leave this item blank.

Mortgages: Show the *principal* balance (not any interest) of all mortgages.

Other Debts: This category is a catch-all and includes medical bills, any unfulfilled pledges to charitable organizations, any unpaid legal judgment.

Again, don't show normal operating expenses here. Add up all your debts and obligations and put the sum under TOTAL LIABILITIES. Next, subtract TOTAL LIABILITIES from TOTAL ASSETS: the result is your NET WORTH. Then add TOTAL LIABILITIES to NET WORTH to give LIABILITIES and NET WORTH which should equal TOTAL ASSETS. Now you can celebrate (we hope).

What you just did while calculating your net worth is figure out the absolute maximum amount of cash you can lay your hands on if you get rid of everything you own and owe. The chances of your doing that are next to zero, but you now have an idea of sources you can tap for your business needs. If you're a year or even two away from buying a business, you'll have to update your net worth statement; but once you've done it the first time, subsequent calculations are a piece of cake.

Now that you know something about your net worth, you need to estimate your monthly living expenses. Determining how much money you need to live on is a vital step, not just an academic exercise. Too many people tell us they're willing to live in a hovel, eat curds and whey, and drive a ten-year-old car to get into their own business. Although some may make adjustments here and there, most people who adopt a certain lifestyle maintain that lifestyle. You don't put yourself in a position of extreme personal sacrifice. A business should provide a certain standard of living and if it doesn't, you may feel that the whole escapade isn't worth the time and effort. We said earlier that good entrepreneurs don't pursue personal wealth as an end product, but they do understand economic values. If a business can't pay you a salary that permits an acceptable lifestyle, then it's not a business, it's a hobby. If it's your *only* source of income under those circumstances, you'll never be satisfied with it.

Use the form provided (Figure 4-2) to estimate your current monthly expenses. Even though you don't plan to be in business for a while, fill it out now

ESTIMATED MONTHLY EXPENSES

Item	Amount
Food	$
Housing	
a. Monthly payment or rent	
b. Taxes	
c. Insurance	
d. Repairs and maintenance	
Clothing	
Auto	
a. Payment	
b. Gasoline	
c. Repairs	
d. Insurance, fees, taxes	
Utilities	
a. Electricity	
b. Heat, hot water (if not electric)	
c. Telephone	
d. Other (water, gas)	
Credit cards (not covered elsewhere)	
Installment and other loans	
Life insurance	
Travel and entertainment	
Donations	
Medical and dental	
Investment and savings	
Miscellaneous	
TOTAL	$

Figure 4-2

to give yourself an idea of your present expenses. In Chapter Eight we'll show you how to do a business plan, and how much you plan to take from the business is one of the items that goes into the financial part of the plan. Banks and other financial sources get turned off if you show little or no compensation for yourself; if you don't plan for a decent wage to meet your needs in the beginning, you may never get the business to the point where it can provide one.

The monthly expenses statement is self-explanatory; however, remember you have to adjust some expenses to get them on a monthly basis. For instance, if your average food bill is \$60 per week, you need to multiply by 4⅓, or 4.33, to reflect a monthly rate:

$$\$60 \times 4.33 = \$260/\text{month}$$

Similarly, if your real estate taxes are \$1200 annually, monthly that expense is:

$$\frac{\$1200}{12} = \$100/\text{month}$$

Now let's summarize what you've discovered about your finances and what it tells you about your ability to purchase a business. Your net worth statement tells you the maximum amount of money you could raise from your personal assets, even though it's highly unlikely you'd want to convert all of them. It's a good idea to earmark those assets that can be readily converted to cash as well as those you're *willing* to convert. That represents your personal investment in the business. Your own personal needs, as expressed in the monthly expense analysis, directly affects what you need to take from a business to support your lifestyle.

By being aware of both of these values, you create a solid foundation of financial information from which to evaluate a prospective business purchase relative to your needs as a buyer and an operator. The net worth statement helps the seller understand your position, just as his or her financial data increases your knowledge of the business. And finally, both the net worth statement and your monthly expense analysis are necessary to complete your business plan and to apply for any loans you may need from a bank.

USING PROFESSIONALS

You may need the services of professionals—accountants, attorneys, consultants—in your search for and purchase of a small business as well as your operation of it. For example, an accountant can help you analyze the financial soundness of a possible purchase. Or you may want an attorney to look at the legal aspects of the business, especially if there are lawsuits against it which may affect you. An attorney can also help draw up the purchase and sale agreement or aid in the formation of a corporation for your new business.

However, there is something you should keep in mind about lawyers and accountants. They're not entrepreneurially minded; if they were, they wouldn't be lawyers and accountants. The safest answer they can give is *not* to buy the business. Too many buyers of small businesses expect an accountant or an attorney to make the decision for them, or to give the business their blessing. The good ones won't. Let the accountant and the attorney render *opinions* on the numbers and the legalities if the deal gets to that stage. When you buy a used car you might hire a lawyer to look over the paperwork or an accountant to doublecheck the financing, but you don't expect them to tell you whether or not the brakes or transmission are sound. The same is true when you're buying a used business. Use professionals as professionals in their area of specialization. Don't expect them to know everything!

SELECTING YOUR ADVISORS

Because your primary outside advisors are your accountant and your attorney, we can't stress strongly enough how important they are especially if your knowledge of financial matters and business law is limited. Yes, they're expensive; their rates may run to $100 an hour, but if they save you money in the long run, their fees are well worth it. Of course, the opposite is true as well; poor ones waste both your time and your money and may even create problems for you. How can you find good advisors? Ask small business owners, the local chamber of commerce, your bank, before you hire. Look for individuals in sole practice or with very small firms. Don't automatically go to the largest accounting or law firm; you may pay more and get less personal service. When you visit your accountant and attorney, tell them about you and your plans to buy a business. Normally the first visit to these professionals is free; if either charges you, you'd be wise to look for another one. *You* interview *them.* Ask about their past experiences with business purchases. Inquire about rates. Once you're satisfied with their technical competence, make sure you like them as people and can communicate easily with them.

YOUR ACCOUNTANT

Many people confuse bookkeeping with accounting. The former consists primarily of writing numbers in such a way that proper records are kept. Bookkeeping is an intermediate step in the creation of the financial statements used to analyze the performance of a business. We recommend small business owners do their own books. You can use the forms and methods suggested in Kamaroff's *Small-Time Operator,** or you can purchase one of the Ideal books from your local bookstore or office supply business. If your business is very simple, your checkbook can suffice as long as you carefully record where your business receipts come from and what your checks (disbursements) are written for. Don't hire an accountant to do bookkeeping.

We highly recommend you look for a *certified public* accountant or CPA. Yes, you'll pay more but you'll get an individual with a broader background and more expertise. A good CPA usually recommends you begin by having him or her prepare your annual personal and business tax reports. When they do your taxes, they will probably want to review the business with you. In this early period, a CPA can also help you with the preparation of financial statements for a bank loan and furnish you with quarterly or monthly statements.

Our advice is: Listen to your accountant. You're paying for what this professional knows and is able to tell you. Notice that we said listen. That doesn't necessarily mean obey. The one problem we find with accountants is that they often give advice only from a financial standpoint, and that's not necessarily the same as from a business view. For example, suppose your accountant tells you the location of your pro-

* *Small-Time Operator: How to Start Your Own Small Business, Keep Your Books, Pay Your Taxes, and Stay Out of Trouble* by Bernard Kamaroff, CPA. Bell Springs Publishing, Box 640, Laytonville, CA 95454.

posed business acquisition is terrible and you should look in another part of town. If you've done careful research and feel it's a good location for you, then looking elsewhere may not necessarily be good advice.

YOUR ATTORNEY

Use the same degree of care when selecting an attorney. Find one who is knowledgeable and personable: someone you can ask a question and get a reasonably straight answer from. Lawyers, like accountants, tend to be a conservative lot, but this is probably to your advantage. When you're buying or operating a business in a country that passes 30,000 laws a year, you don't want to be dealing with a gun-slinger. Be sure to select an attorney with business experience, not one who specializes in domestic suits and divorces or in criminal law. If you can't locate one by word of mouth, write to the state bar association or get a copy of *Martindale-Hubbel,* a national directory of lawyers and law firms showing professional specialties, from your library.

Expect to use an attorney to form a corporation, draft a partnership agreement, examine legal documents (that is, a lease), and draw up employment contracts. When you're in business, you can also (and unfortunately) expect to eventually be a party to a court action, whether you initiate it or not. A lawyer can't *prevent* you from being sued, but you need one if you're named in a suit of one kind or another.

Remember, a good attorney won't make decisions for you. The good ones present options and advise regarding what they believe to be your best course of action, but the final decision is yours. Also, remember what we said about taking *business* advice from lawyers; most of them understand the legal implications of business but few understand business itself.

OTHER ADVISORS

Of course, anyone can be an advisor to you, including your mother. If the lady has business experience, fine; but if not, you'll find out all over again what being polite really means. What we mean by advisors are people who have an interest in small business. One very trusted advisor is your banker if you have one. Get one thing straight from the beginning: Bankers aren't the enemy. While it's true many bankers have never been through what you're doing, they talk with many would-be business owners and observe many small businesses. Because they've also been involved in some business failures, they may have some very valuable advice for you, especially about the local climate.

Visit your local Small Business Administration (SBA) office and ask to see one of the management assistance officers. Go over your ideas with that person and listen to what he or she has to say. Remember, you don't have to follow their advice, but you should pay attention. The officer might recommend you see someone from either their SCORE (Service Corps of Retired Executives) or ACE (Active Corps of Executives) programs. The service of these people is free, but you have to pay their travel expenses. One SBA service that seems to work well is the Small Business Development Centers (SBDCs) established at colleges and universities to help local residents and businesses. In some instances the advice you get from consultants at the SBDCs is free; in other cases you pay a fee.

There are also private consultants who specialize in small business. They charge from $25 to $60 per hour, and, unlike lawyers or CPAs, have no minimum educational or experience requirements or qualifying exams. If you use consultants, be certain to check them out in advance. If they're good at what they do, buying a few hours of their time is well worth the cost.

Don't overlook the best advisors—other business owners. Most of them will feel flattered to talk with you. You might even be able to talk openly with the owner of the same kind of business you're considering. If you find uncooperative owners, politely excuse yourself. Chances are those people are operating out of some kind of fear and you wouldn't find their advice helpful anyway.

And don't forget your business broker if you are using one. You can expect that person to have skill and expertise you can tap, too.

Some business buyers try to do everything themselves—form a new corporation, set up their books, select their own types of insurance coverage. While we see businesses for which the new business owner can do all these successfully—a small service business for example—those situations are the exception rather than the rule. We urge you to use advisors if you have little or no experience in these various areas. These people will more than likely save you far more than their services cost. For those of you who believe you'll save money by doing everything yourself, our question is, "What's your own time worth?"

Chapter FIVE

Preliminary Investigations

By now you've probably already ruled out those businesses that are obviously poor choices. Some get knocked out of the running immediately because they're not the kind of business you're looking for. Others may not appeal to you for a number of reasons—physical condition of the premises, location, surly or uncooperative seller, price far out of range. Other businesses simply may not feel right. That's an intuitive judgment, but trust your feelings; they're every bit as important as all the analysis.

In the next two chapters we're going to explore different techniques for evaluating the seller and the business. The object is to determine whether a business is the right one for you; buying the wrong business has many more implications than taking the wrong job. Spend the time to do your looking and analysis with care. Don't be rushed by anyone—not a broker, spouse, seller, or yourself. If a good business is sold to someone else before you complete your investigations and preparations, that's the nature of the world. If you aren't thoroughly prepared to buy the business, there's a real good chance you're not prepared to run it, either.

Let's assume it's time to meet the seller and look at the business for the first time. You may have had a phone conversation with the seller, or a broker may have shown you some preliminary information, but so far no face-to-face encounter has occurred. But now it's time to visit the business location and the seller, a visit that can teach you a great deal.

GUT FEELINGS AND NEIGHBORHOODS

We have yet to see a business sell without the buyer's seeing the business first. If it were just a matter of wanting to buy a business that's profitable, the buyer could look at the books and other data on the business and buy or not buy it based on that information.

But buyers always want to see the business, and not just to inspect the equipment; they want to get a "feel" for the business. Everything about that business may check out fine, but if you're uncomfortable there, if the vibes aren't right or there's just something about it that doesn't click—don't buy it! Buying a business is as much a result of gut feeling as the data presented in the business's books and records.

The neighborhood (location) of the business is also very important. Some businesses are specialty types that draw people from all over, whereas others depend on the people in the immediate area for their survival. Every neighborhood probably has an ice cream store, but how many stores are there that sell ice cream-making equipment? Not many. There are a lot of bookstores, but how many specialize in books on magic? Or, how about the auto parts store that specializes in Corvette parts? These types of specialty businesses draw people from miles around because customers can't buy these products anyplace else. In these cases, neighborhood isn't important to the suscess of the business, but your personal reaction to the neighborhood is.

If you're not comfortable there, the business probably won't fit you no matter what. Specialty businesses, however, can be moved to another location more readily than neighborhood types. If you're looking at a neighborhood-dependent business and you don't like the neighborhood, your chances of succeeding are slim.

Once you drive all around the neighborhood, park somewhere near the business. Don't park in the business parking lot unless there's no other choice (if it's located in a shopping center or mall for example). Walk around the immediate area and look at surrounding businesses if there are any. Observe customers of these businesses. What kind of businesses surround the one you're considering? What are the people like? What kind of hours do these stores keep? (Hours are usually posted on the front door or near it.) Now, walk by the business you're visiting. Check the appearance, the signs. Look at everything you can see from the outside before you go in.

MEETING WITH THE SELLER

There are a few things to keep in mind about meeting with the seller. More than likely the seller is going to try and sell you the business. Even if he's not a salesman, he'll become one now. The simple fact that you agree to the appointment marks you as a "live one." Sellers are usually their own worst enemy; they tend to oversell, showing you the new stainless steel equipment that will make you millions. They tell you about the factory across the street whose new third shift will make you a fortune if you stay open 24 hours a day. By the time they're done, the asking price is ten million dollars and a steal at double the price.

Before you get defensive, remember the last house you sold; didn't you tell the real estate broker or the prospective buyer about all its wonderful features? It's a natural thing to do.

When you meet the seller, he or she will give you a price, and that price will most likely be all cash and very high. Don't faint, don't panic and don't let on that you're ready to pass out! Don't let the seller intimidate you with an exorbitant price or terms; and don't be discouraged. Consider it all part of your education.

Now that we know sellers tend to oversell and ask for outlandish prices or terms, let's go inside the business. Once inside, introduce yourself and state your purpose; for example, "I'm Joe Jones, and I have an appointment to see Harry Brown." The employee may go get the owner or usher you to the owner. Or, perhaps the employee is the owner. In any case, you are now in front of the seller, who says something like, "What do you want to know?" And there you are—caught off guard. Rather than launch into a lot of questions right off, ask the seller if there's a place where you can talk for a few minutes. Most businesses do have places that offer a degree of privacy, even if it's just a booth or a table in a restaurant or the seller's office. If there isn't such a place, ask the seller if you can buy him or her a cup of coffee and go to the nearest coffee shop or restaurant.

Once you're settled, this kind of typical conversation between you and the seller is likely to occur:

YOU: "Nice place you have here. How much business do you do?"

SELLER: "What do you mean?"

YOU: "Well, how much business did you do last year?" (If he still has trouble understanding, and don't kid yourself, he knows exactly what you are asking, ask him how much he does in a month or a week.)

SELLER: "We do about $8,000 a month."

YOU: "What are you asking for the business?"

SELLER: "How much do you think it's worth?" (He knows what he wants for it; he's testing you.)

YOU: "I'm just looking and I'm not really a good judge of what a business like this sells for. I'm sure you have some idea of how much you want for your business."

SELLER: "Well, the business is worth at least $75,000. I'd let it go for that plus inventory."

YOU: "What kind of terms are you giving?"

SELLER: "Terms—what do you mean terms! I've got to have all cash; I'm moving to Florida—I want to buy a business down there. I'm going to need cash to do that."

YOU: "Oh, I just thought most businesses sold for so much down and then so much a month." (It's okay to play a little bit dumb.)

SELLER: "What do you think I am, a bank?"

YOU: "No. I just wanted to know if you would consider terms." (You won the point—drop it.) "So you're going to Florida—how long have you been here?" (This is a key question so pay close attention to the answer.)

SELLER: "Ten years—going on eleven."

YOU: "How come you're moving to Florida?" (The shorter the time the owner's been in business, the more important this answer is.)

SELLER: "My wife says if I don't get her out of the cold this year, she's going without me. I'm going to try and buy the same kind of business down there."

YOU: "You must really like it. By the way, how much could I make out of a business like this?"

SELLER: "Oh, about $25,000 a year."

YOU: "Do your books show that?"

SELLER: "Oh yeah, but the books don't show everything!" (laughs)

Repeat the information the seller has given you to be sure you understand.

YOU: "Let me see, you're asking $75,000 for your business, right?"

SELLER: "Yeah."

YOU: "And you're doing about $8,000 a month gross and make about $25,000 a year."

SELLER: "That's about right."

YOU: "And, you've been here about ten years. Did you start the business or buy it from somebody else?"

SELLER: "Oh, no, this place has been here for at least 20 years—that I know of."

YOU: "What's the rent?"

SELLER: "$650 a month."

YOU: "What's that include?"

SELLER: "What do you mean?"

YOU: "Does that $650 cover taxes, heat. . . . ?"

SELLER: "Oh, I get it. It includes everything, even the water. I pay the utilities and the insurance on my equipment, but not on the building. Is that what you mean?"

YOU: "Yes. How long is your lease?"

SELLER: "Well, let's see, I signed a new lease two years ago so I have about three years left. It's a five-year lease." (It's important that you find out the lease information. If the seller has a five-year lease, but he's used up 4½ years of it, you need to know that. And although you're not buying the place yet, now's the time to get the facts. We'll talk more about leases in Chapter Six.)

YOU: "Is there an option on the lease?" (An option is merely a right to extend the lease by the tenant. It either specifies what the rent will be or gives the tenant the right to extend the lease for a period of time for a rent to be negotiated at the time the option is exercised.)

SELLER: "It's a five-year option. At the end of five years the rent goes up $150 per month. I've got my lease right here—do you want to see it?"

YOU: "Yes, I'd like to take a quick look." (This is part of your education. You may not understand much of it, but it shows the seller you're interested and you have to get familiar with leases sometime.) "Thanks. How come you don't post your hours on the door?"

SELLER: "I used to, but I change them a lot. Now I'm open from 10:00 A.M. to 6:00 P.M." (He's telling you something important, isn't he? A good business doesn't change hours a lot.) "And, I'm closed on Sunday."

YOU: "Oh, what were your hours?"

SELLER: "I used to be open from 9:00 A.M. to 8:00 P.M. but it was too much work and I was always tired, so I cut back." (See the things you can find out? Now you know his business may be down because of the shorter hours and that he's tired and probably wants out of the business. This means the financial records may not be the whole story and that his take-it-or-leave-it attitude may not reflect his true feelings.)

YOU: "Do you own everything in here?"

SELLER: "Yeah, I own everything, free and clear. I don't owe a dime." (Remember this; it's important.)

YOU: "I don't want to see the books now, but you think they show about $8,000 a month in gross sales and a yearly net of about $25,000?"

SELLER: "At least that. I don't put everything on my books, you know." (Now he's opening up a little more. This is the second time he's mentioned the books didn't show everything.)

YOU: "I know you said you want all cash, but would you consider terms?"

SELLER: "What do you mean terms?"

YOU: "I mean, how much down would you take?"

SELLER: "I don't know; I'm going to need as much money as possible for the Florida move. Make me an offer! What do you think?" (See how quickly a seller may react to anyone who's really interested in buying?)

YOU: That depends on how much of a monthly payment I'd have." (Now, you're both pushing a little. Back off—you got enough information and education for one visit.)

SELLER: "I don't know. I'll have to give that some thought."

YOU: "Well, thanks a lot—you have a nice business here. Oh, by the way, are you the only owner or do you have a partner?"

SELLER: "No, I own it—it's just me and the wife."

YOU: "Thanks a lot for your time. You've given me a lot of information and I want to give it some thought. If I have more questions, can I usually find you here?"

SELLER: "Yes, I'm almost always here except Saturdays. I don't work Saturdays, unless my help doesn't show." (Another little bit of information. He doesn't work weekends. It's these little pieces of information that really tell you about the owner and the way he conducts his business.)

YOU: "Fine. Well, good-bye and thanks again."

Even if you're really interested in the business, your first meeting is over. Don't get into the money or the books or the detailed analysis at this point. Don't overstay your welcome; the seller does have a business to run. Furthermore, sometimes things are said in idle conversation that can damage your future negotiations.

Before you leave, the seller may open his desk drawer and throw profit and loss statements at you. If he does, tell him you'll examine them at a later time. Sellers who open their records for you are telling you, at least on the surface, they have nothing to hide.

After you leave the business, repeat the earlier steps. Walk around the area and slowly drive through the neighborhood again. The more interested you are in the business, the more scouting you should do. Also, fill out a form like the one below on this page. Anything that strikes you as odd or those things you don't understand should be put in the notes. For example, this business had a five-year lease with an option; you might want to remind yourself to find out more about leases. Or you might want to jot down a few comments about the seller's references to his books not giving the whole financial picture; does that mean you're looking at a crooked business? All these impressions are important and easily forgotten or confused when you visit more than one business. Take a few minutes to fill out the form after you leave the seller so you'll be sure your information is as accurate as possible.

On the way home, look at the other businesses you pass. Now that you're fairly familiar with one business, you can look at every business with an eye towards ownership, price, terms, gross sales, and profits. Once you visit the first business with the idea of possibly buying it, suddenly all businesses take on new meaning for you. Now you can easily imagine that that business you pass every day that's always appealed to you could be *your* business. Or, perhaps there's a business you always patronize that really turns you on; you wonder what it would be like to own it. Now that you're beginning the process of looking for a business, investigate all possibilities—if only to further your education.

Once you're back home, arrange your information. You may talk to many sellers and you need to organize the information for easy comparison. Let's look at three important factors: (1) how long the business has been in existence, (2) how long the seller has owned it, and (3) the reason for the sale.

Name of Business ______________________

Type of Business ______________________

Seller's Name ______________________

Address ______________________

Telephone Number ______________________

Monthly Sales ______________________

Monthly Profit ______________________

Asking Price ______________________

Down Payment ______________________

Inventory Included? ______________ Amount ______________

Years in Business ______________ Business Established ______________

Hours and Days Open ______________________

Reason for Sale ______________________

NOTES:

RATING A BUSINESS

Let's use a scale from one to ten to record how long a business has been in existence.

Scale	
10 or more	
9	
8	
7	
6	Number of years the business has been in existence
5	
4	
3	
2	
1 or less	

The longer a small business operates, the greater its chance of survival. As a business survives and ages, it creates more and more momentum of its own. This means that a business with an established track record can more readily absorb the early mistakes new owners invariably make.

In general, the longer the seller has owned the business, the better. Notice we said in general. If a business owner fails to keep up with changes over a long period, the business could be on its way out. For example, if a large part of the income of Joe's Sportarama came from sales and maintenance of snowmobiles during the past ten years but the owners of the high-priced condominiums that surround his store now prefer cross-country skiing, Joe's business could be in danger. Keeping such possibilities in mind, rate any businesses you visit using the same zero-to-ten scale.

Scale	
10 or more	
9	
8	
7	
6	Number of years the seller has owned the business
5	
4	
3	
2	
1 or less	

The third key indicator is why the owner wants to sell the business. If he's been there for 20 years, is 67 years old and wants to retire—that's a good reason. If he's been there six months, is 45, and wants to sell because he's sick, you need to know what he's sick of. It's certainly possible he has a serious disease and therefore should be selling, but nine out of ten times he's sick of the business. *The* REAL *reason for the sale is probably the single most important factor to know before buying a small business.* Many of the businesses put up for sale every year are "distressed" merchandise. They may be attractive, well located, and appear to have everything going for them, except they don't seem to make very much money. It's possible and very likely that new management could change these businesses, but it's much more of a gamble for a first-time business buyer.

Most of these distressed businesses have been owned by the sellers for 18 months or less, and the owners have some very interesting reasons for putting these businesses up for sale. Our favorite is the guy who put his business on the market after six months because now "It's too far to drive from home to work." You'd think he'd have thought of that before he bought the business. Better get the real reason!

If the reason for the sale just doesn't make sense, find out the real reason. Often the seller just isn't making a go of it. The financial information will tell you this; ask to see it. If the real reason is that the business is failing, eliminate the business from your list. However, if you really feel you can turn the business around, you now know the price is very negotiable.

How do you go about finding out the real reason if you think the seller's withholding some information? Let's look at an example. Suppose a seller says his wife has arthritis and he wants to sell his great lunch business and move to a milder climate. On several occasions during the week, you drive by the place at lunch time and there doesn't seem to be much of a crowd. It's time to confront the owner:

> "Mr. Seller, I can understand why your wife wants to move to a warmer climate, and that's the reason you want to sell your business, but I've driven by on three or four occasions at lunch time and it doesn't seem too busy."

Then wait for an answer. He may have a valid reason; maybe the factories that normally provide his lunch business are closed for two weeks' vacation, or maybe they're on strike. It may also be because he just doesn't have a very good business. Or maybe he's only been there a month or two—and it's still a good business, but he's not a good businessman. Some people just aren't cut out to own a business, and they find this out very shortly and try to sell it.

Let's look at some other commonly given reasons that need further explanation. If the buyer says that he or she has to sell for health reasons, find out the nature of the illness. If there are family problems, how serious are they? If Molly wants to sell Molly's Ice Cream Shop and retire, find out how old Molly is and if she can really afford to retire. If a spouse is being transferred, make sure he doesn't just want to transfer the business and its problems to you. If the seller claims that he's tired, make sure that he's not just tired of making ends meet.

Remember, the reason for the sale may sound fishy to you, but it can be very real to the seller. For example, even the best, most successful coffee shop owner could get tired after getting up at 4:00 A.M. seven days a week for ten years to bake those famous doughnuts. After such a schedule, wanting to drive a school bus may not seem like such an odd reason to sell—especially if he has kids he never saw while he was running that business. That's why the length of time the business has been owned is so important. The reason for sale can also give you an idea how fast the seller wants or needs to sell the business. If he's tired, he may prefer to be tired for a long time rather than reduce his price or give terms. On the other hand, if his family is really pushing him to spend more time at home or he realizes the damage being done to his relationship with them or his health exceeds anything he could gain from hanging on to the business, he may jump at any offer.

The reason for sale really determines how quickly the seller wants out of the business, which usually determines the price and terms. Obviously, the quicker he wants out of the business, the better the price and the terms. For example, Paul is a charming 74-year-old restaurant owner who's owned the same business at the same location for 40 years where he still works every day. When Paul said he was tired and wanted to get out of the business and retire, all he said he wanted was the money for his fixtures, equipment, and inventory. The fixtures and equipment have been there since Paul opened, and they aren't worth more than $20,000; his inventory is only about $10,000 at any one time. He doesn't have a liquor license, only beer and wine. His is an ethnic restaurant—not in the best part of town, but it provides him with a very good living because of its unique food. He still goes to the market to buy the meat and the vegetables, this 74-year-old, amazing man. However, when it actually got down to selling the restaurant, when Paul had to let go, he couldn't do it. All of a sudden he decided the place was worth several hundred thousand dollars. Paul wasn't a willing seller; in fact, he wasn't a seller at all.

If the seller doesn't really want to sell the business, chances are the conditions surrounding the sale will be fixed and inflexible. For example, Paul's main reason for selling was because his children had told him someone his age shouldn't be working so hard. Because Paul enjoyed the work, that reason simply wasn't enough to let him give up something that meant so much to him. Rather than tell his children he disagreed with them, he simply priced his business out of the market.

The more a seller wants out, the more flexible he or she will be in giving you price and terms and room for negotiation. If it's a real emergency, such as a pending divorce or a very serious illness, then the price and terms, or at least the seller's willingness to be flexible on the price, are on your side. Rate the reason for sale to determine how willing a seller may be, using the scale below.

9–10

10 • Court-ordered divorce sale
• Fatal illness
9 • Estate sale
8 • Spouse transferred

7–8

• Partner problems (legal)
7 • Serious illness/accident
• Divorce
6 • Retirement (real)

5–6

• Wants larger business
5 • Spouse problems
• Illness/accident
4 • Moving out of area

3–4

3 • Too many other interests
• Moving within area
• Tired of business
2 • Employee problems

1–2

1 • Business can't support seller
• Major problems with business
• Suspected false reason for sale
• Business closed (pro only)

You now have three numerical ratings. Take a look at each one separately and then average them. Suppose you look at the business that's been around for seven years, with the seller running it for the last five. The seller wants a larger business. The average rating for that business is:

$$\begin{array}{rl} 7 & \text{(age of business)} \\ 5 & \text{(number years seller has owned it)} \\ \underline{6} & \text{(reason for sale)} \\ 18 & \end{array}$$

$$\frac{18}{3} = 6 \text{ (average rating)}$$

Now rate the business overall, using this scale:

9–10 : excellent
7–8 : good
5–6 : average
3–4 : poor
1–2 : very poor (for a pro *only*)

Our business, like most of the businesses you will see, is average. Notice that those whose reasons for sale or overall rating is 1–2 are recommended as potential businesses *only* for those with proven business skills. These are definitely *not* prospects for first-time business owners.

HOW LONG ON THE MARKET IS TOO LONG?

Another factor to think about when deciding whether a business is worth further consideration is how long the business has been for sale. However, the seller may not want to tell you this, but if you say,

> "Mr. Seller, how long have you been trying to sell this business?"

and he replies:

> "Oh, just a few weeks or so."

you don't know any more than when you started.

Going through the old classified business opportunities ads at the local newspaper office might show you he or the broker have been advertising this business for some time. Buyers, sellers, and brokers seem to be concerned about how long a business has been on the market. If it's a good business, it sells overnight. Because it doesn't, it must be a bad business, right? Not always. If the seller knows he has a real dog on his hands, he may price it for a quick sale; he'll do whatever it takes to get out of the business. The owner who feels he has a pretty good business may be a bit tougher in his approach. He may start out with too high a price, may not be willing to accept a reasonable down payment, or may be asking all cash. He may really want to sell, but feels he doesn't want to give it away.

It often takes time for such a seller to come down to earth. Remember Paul, the 74-year-old owner of the ethnic restaurant? Well, he's selling his sweat and blood; that business *is* his life. Unfortunately, nobody will pay him for that. Buyers will tell him his business isn't worth what he is asking, or they may offer half of what he's asking. *If* he wants to sell, he'll have to lower his sights considerably. Unfortunately, if you're the first to make an offer on his business, it may get rejected. However, that same offer could get accepted six months later. For example, suppose six months after Paul sets his exorbitant price on his restaurant to satisfy his kids, an old friend asks him to buy the other half of a duplex in the Indiana town they grew up in. Now all of a sudden Paul has what he considers a *good* reason to sell his business, and he's much more willing to negotiate. In this case the buyer of a business that's been for sale a long time could get a pretty good deal.

THE KICKED-AROUND BUSINESS

You do want to avoid businesses that have been kicked around, those that sell two or three times a year. For some reason these particular businesses never click. They may be in a doomed location or have some other fatal flaw. Many times the only flaw you can spot is that the business is a kick-around; but that's more than enough reason to eliminate it from your list. Even the pros have trouble making these yo-yos work.

Before we leave this chapter, let's say a few words about the tough and/or all cash seller. Sellers who refuse to budge on the price or insist that the price be paid in cash may just be stubborn. However, this stubbornness may be hiding a very good business; many times the tougher the seller, the better the business person he or she is and the better the business. They know a lot more about that business than you do, and as we'll learn in the next chapter, there may be a lot more to the business than there appears. That's why owners of such businesses can afford to be tough sellers. If the seller is completely unreasonable, that's one thing; but if the seller is just hanging in for price and terms, don't be too quick to dismiss the business if you like it.

Chapter SIX

Analyzing Business Opportunities

REVIEW

Let's pause here in our discussion of the process for acquiring a business with a minimum of risk and review where we've been together. Then we'll outline where we're going from here.

We discussed what it takes to get into your own business, lifestyle, various categories of business, where to look for opportunities, some initial considerations about gathering information on the business, your own finances, how to select and use professionals, and your first conversation with the seller. At this stage you've ruled out the obvious poor choices, and learned to trust your intuition as well as your logic.

You're now in a new phase in your quest for your own business; now the work really begins, but don't see it as drudgery or even frightening. Investigation, analysis, and negotiation can be fun and interesting when it's about something that can benefit you directly.

By now you should have a few businesses you want to analyze further. This means you'll gather more information from the seller (or a broker will gather it for you) and from other sources as well. Then your next task is to analyze that information and the proper price and terms for the business and present your conclusions to the seller. From these negotiations you can probably zero in on one business, but there are a few more things to do before you go to the closing, pay your money, and take your chances.

In this chapter we'll cover some of the techniques for assessing the strengths and weaknesses of a business. All businesses have weak points, and it's better to discover them before you take over. After you evaluate the business you may decide it has too many flaws for you to tackle; or you may see strengthening those weak areas as a challenge. Remember: if you're a first-time buyer, be a bit cautious about getting into a business that needs lots of work to put it right. Save that one for your second or third purchase.

THE BUSINESS—AN EXTERNAL VIEW

Before Ray Kroc approached two brothers named McDonald at their hamburger stand in California to make them a deal they couldn't refuse, he spent several days in his car simply watching the business. Only when he was sure the place and the concept were both profitable and intriguing did he make his move. The result was McDonald's; the rest is history.

You can benefit from Kroc's approach. Spend a day or two observing the business. Get an idea of the kinds of customers frequenting the business; find out what they like and dislike about the business, its product or service, and the present owner.

It's important to pay a lot of attention to the market or customers the business serves as well as its competition. Many people believe businesses fail because they run out of money. That's like saying a thief shot during a holdup attempt died because his heart stopped. Both statements are true as far as they go, but both also fail to address the real problem.

Rule: Most businesses fail because of a marketing flaw.

What do we mean by a marketing flaw? A marketing flaw means the business and the customers aren't properly matched. Here are some typical marketing flaws:

- Too much competition.
- The image the business portrays isn't what it delivers—what you see ain't what you get.
- The owner doesn't create enough awareness of the business through advertising and promotion.
- Prices are out of line with the type of business, nature of the market, or number and type of competitors.
- The business has no Unique Selling Proposition (USP).
- The sales and distribution methods aren't effective.
- Customer service is poor or non-existent.
- Credit policies are too lax, allowing accounts receivable to build up.

Spend most of your effort outside the business, concerning yourself with marketing factors. Find out about the business's reputation. Take a look at the competition or have someone else, possibly a consultant, do it for you. If your candidate is a retail or service establishment, have some friends go there and buy something. Ask them what they think.

If you see a pattern emerging that sends up those little warning signals, back out of the deal unless there's some other darn good reason not to. Remember, there are lots of businesses for sale, lots of good ones at fair prices.

THE BUSINESS—AN INTERNAL VIEW

You'll be depending on the owner for much of the inside information, and business owners are human beings like the rest of us. Once most owners discover you're serious and qualified (meaning you really want your own business and have the cash to buy it), they'll willingly go over all the details of the business with you. It's in their best interest, and most sellers realize falsifying information can come back to haunt them in the form of a lawsuit.

Remember, if you run across a seller who isn't open and forthright, back off; let someone else go through the hassle of prying information loose. If you're dealing through a business broker, he or she can be the one to get the information for you.

In this section we're going to deal with the analysis of operational data—information about what goes on in the business. By examining the business this way, you discover the strengths and weaknesses of the business; then you can decide if you want to keep going.

We've included a business analysis checklist to give you an idea what kinds of questions to ask. Some of the areas may not apply to the business you're looking at. If that's the case, simply eliminate these questions.

Notice the business analysis checklist is similar to the skills checklist you completed in Chapter Two. You may find it helpful to compare the two after you analyze a business to point up areas where there may be a dual weakness. For example, suppose you note in the skills checklist that your knowledge of pricing is weak or nonexistent and your analysis of the business shows that pricing is an area that need attention. This means you need to increase your knowledge of pricing or bring in an accountant or business consultant to help you if you purchase that business.

BUSINESS ANALYSIS CHECKLIST

Based upon my analysis of the business, I believe that the operation is currently being run satisfactorily.

Item	Consideration	Yes	No	?	Notes
I. SALES AND MARKETING					
A. Pricing	Is markup in line with current industry practice and/or competition so that there is a profit?				
B. Market Research	Has the business taken advantage of market potential? Has competition been analyzed?				
C. Market Planning	Has the business taken advantage of market opportunities?				
D. Personal Selling	Does the current owner use good, honest selling techniques?				
E. Customer Service	Is there the proper balance between serving the customers' needs and good business practice?				
F. Advertising and Public Relations	Does the business use media in terms of a good balance? Does the amount spent make sense with the level of business and its growth?				
G. Sales Management	Are salespersons and outside agents properly directed in their duties?				
II. BUSINESS OPERATIONS					
A. Purchasing	Are reputable, competitive vendors used? Is there a purchasing program?				
B. Inventory Control	Is slow-moving stock (or materials) managed?				
C. Scheduling	Do goods and materials move through the business without tie-ups and problems?				
D. Quality Control	Are inferior incoming materials rejected and sent back to the suppliers? Are customers satisfied with the current product?				
E. Business Growth	Has the business grown at least above the rate of inflation?				
F. Site Location	Is the present location a beneficial one?				
G. Insurance	Are reasonable risks to the business covered?				
III. FINANCIAL					
A. Bookkeeping and Accounting	Are the books of the company adequate? Are records easy to obtain?				
B. Budgeting	Is a cash flow budget used?				
C. Cost Control	Are cost items managed and efforts applied to keep high-cost items under control?				
D. Raising Money	Has the current owner(s) been successful in raising capital when it's needed?				

BUSINESS ANALYSIS CHECKLIST

Item	Consideration	Yes	No	?	Notes
E. Credit and Collection	Is the current C & C policy adequate for today's needs?				
F. Dealing with Banks	Is the relationship between the business owner and his/her banker open and friendly?				
G. Cost of Money	When loans were taken out, were the interest rate and the loan conditions appropriate?				
H. Specific Areas	Has the current owner shown knowledge of 1. Breakeven analysis? 2. Cash flow? 3. Financial statements? 4. Operating ratios? 5. Taxes?				
IV. PERSONNEL					
A. Hiring	Has the right mix of people been hired? Is turnover high?				
B. Training	Are the employees suitably trained for what they're expected to do?				
C. Motivating People	Do the employees appear to enjoy their work?				
D. Enforcing Policies	Does there seem to be a logical order to what goes on in the business?				
E. Communicating	Do people know what is going on? Are they brought in on decisions?				
V. ADMINISTRATIVE/MANAGEMENT					
A. Record Keeping	Are records of past transactions and events readily available?				
B. Problem Solving	Are there very few unsolved problems?				
C. Decision Making	Is the current owner(s) decisive?				
D. Negotiating	Has the current owner(s) taken advantage of conditions to his/her favor by securing the best available terms?				
E. Government Regulations	Is the current owner(s) aware of local, state, and federal regulations that affect the business?				
F. Leadership	Does the current owner(s) take charge of the business and its employees?				
G. Developing Subordinates	If the current owner(s) were to die suddenly (or become disabled), is there a ready successor?				
H. Business Law	Do current owner(s) show a knowledge of applicable business law-contracts, agency, UCC? Are there contracts in effect that will bind you?				
I. Dealing with Professionals	Does the business use an accountant, attorney, consultant? Can you use them also?				

THE LEASE

One very important item to analyze is any lease the seller or the seller's corporation has with a landlord. Naturally, if you're buying the real estate (as is the usual case in the sale of a motel, for example), then there is no lease.

Your basic concern is whether you can continue operating the business at its present location under somewhat the same terms and conditions as the seller. Whether or not you can assume the seller's lease is up to the landlord. Therefore, it's important to meet with the landlord and discuss what you're getting into. Sometimes the seller may be reluctant to put you and the landlord together. This may be because the seller doesn't want it publicly known that the business is for sale or because the rent hasn't been paid for a month or two. In these cases you may need to convince the seller you must know about the lease *before* you can consider serious negotiations on price and terms. You also need to know how much rent you'll be paying so you can work it into your financial projections in your business plan (Chapter Eight).

You can either assume a lease or you can't. If the landlord lets you assume the remaining lease, be sure you find out three things:

1. The remaining term of the lease.
2. The amount of the rent.
3. What the rent includes (heat, electricity, etc.)

The landlord might be willing to extend the lease but only if the rent is increased. Be absolutely certain you know how much any increase will be; then check to be sure that amount is reasonable for the size and type of business you're buying.

You often hear lease rates quoted as so much per square foot. This means more to the landlord than it does to you. It's more beneficial for you to relate the amount of rent to a percentage of sales to make sure you're not overpaying. Let's do a brief example. The landlord tells you you can't assume the existing lease but he's willing to sign a new five-year lease covering rent only (you pay utilities) at $6 a square foot. What he means is that the *annual* rent is $6 times the number of square feet being rented. If there are 2,000 square feet, the annual rent is

$$\$6.00 \times 2{,}000 = \$12{,}000$$

or $1,000 per month.

To determine if that's a fair rent based upon annual sales, call an accountant or banker or spend the day in the library (the Robert Morris *Annual Statement Studies* is a good source book for this kind of information) to get the average percentage of sales that fits the type and size of the business you're considering. Most U.S. businesses pay between 3 and 7 percent of their annual sales for rent.

Let's assume you're looking at a hardware store grossing $200,000. Your banker tells you the average rent paid by such establishments in your area is 4 percent of sales. Four percent of $200,000 is $8,000—a lot less than the $12,000 the landlord wants. The percentage he wants is

$$\frac{\$12{,}000}{\$200{,}000} \times 100 = 6\%$$

Better think about looking for another business or moving this one if you're really interested in it.

Some leases are dependent on a percentage of sales. Others have escalation clauses that tie the rent to changes in the cost-of-living index. What you want is the longest term possible with few, if any, increases. However, the landlord wants the shortest term, so you may have to meet somewhere in the middle. Just remember, if you wind up paying too much rent, that rent quite literally takes money out of your pocket and could even cripple the business financially.

THE BUSINESS—A FINANCIAL VIEW

If you get this far, it's time to take a look at finances, the dollars and cents of the enterprise. There are several reasons for doing this:

1. It more thoroughly familiarizes you with the business.
2. It helps you spot other strengths and weaknesses.
3. It tells you whether the business is growing, shrinking, or just holding its own.
4. It helps you determine the proper price for the business.
5. It tells you how much you can expect to make from the business.

You can work with financial information yourself or have an accountant do it for you. If you choose the latter, use your own accountant rather than the seller's.

Many sellers insist on a deposit, called earnest money, before they'll show books, records, statements. Most business brokers insist you make a signed offer on the business in addition to this deposit. However, we feel you can't make an intelligent offer until you look at past financial information. So what do you do about the deposit? If you choose to put up earnest money, be sure you have a written agreement that the deposit will be returned if the financial data shows the business isn't viable for you. If a business broker is handling the transaction, this return agreement is fairly standard practice.

The intent behind deposits is to force you to prove your seriousness and separate sincere prospective buyers from the lookers and curiosity seekers. A broker wants a signed offer because it establishes the price. Many brokers see no point in going through all the paperwork only to discover the buyer and seller can't agree on price. However, don't be pressured to move more quickly than you want.

When you ask the seller for complete financial data, you may get any kind of a response, from total openness to outright refusal. These two extremes are easy to deal with; in the first case you can proceed with your investigations and in the second you simply walk away. Problems occur with the variations in between. Here are a few of the more common intermediate responses:

1. The seller is reluctant to turn information over to you. In most cases when this happens, the seller is unsure exactly what you're going to do with it. He/she fears a breach in confidentiality. If this is the case, assure the seller you'll only show the data to those professionals (accountant, consultant) who are helping you. Another reason for reluctance may occur if the seller thinks you're only window shopping. It's important to stress that you wouldn't ask for financial data if you weren't serious. After all, you're going to spend your time and effort examining the information; that fact alone should be enough to convince most sellers of your sincerity.
2. After your request, the seller leaves the room and returns with a shopping bag full of slips of paper and dumps them on the table. You can't (and shouldn't) do anything with them. If the seller is serious about the sale of the business, he or she should have complete financial statements—income statements and balance sheets—available. Sometimes the only formal records a small business has are its tax returns for past years. If you're familiar with Schedule C of IRS Form 1040 (for proprietorships) or Form 1120 or 1120S (for corporations), you can probably use them. Otherwise you'll need an accountant's help. You'll also need assistance if the seller only gives you checking account statements.
3. The financial information is available but the seller brings up the issue of unreported income—skimming. No one knows for sure how many business owners skim, but the percentage is high. The paradox is that the owner usually does more financial harm than good by pocketing income and not reporting it. This is more than just invoking the ire of the IRS. Unreported income is just that—money that should have shown up either as owner's salary or profit. If reported, it adds to the price of the business. However, because it isn't reported, it has *no* value. Here's the rule:

   NEVER, NEVER pay for skimming!!!

   If the owner tries to adjust the financial data to include the unreported income, tell him/her you can't consider the adjustment valid. If the owner argues and holds firm, walk out of the deal. If an owner's been skimming, it should make you wonder what other illegal practices are part of the business.

What is "complete financial information"? The answer is whatever the seller has. However, for you (or an accountant) to make meaningful judgments, you need three years' worth of

- business income tax returns
- balance sheets (if available)
- supporting information (if applicable)
- income statements.

Unless the tax returns are the only information you get, there's not too much you need to do with them except familiarize yourself with the reporting procedure.

Which of the three most common forms of business is this: a proprietorship, partnership, or corporation? We estimate that half the businesses sold are proprietorships or partnerships (the first being more popular) and the other half are corporations or Subchapter S corporations. A Subchapter S corporation is a small business corporation in which the owners (stockholders) elect to be taxed as a partnership.

THE BALANCE SHEET (AND SUPPORTING INFORMATION)

For most small businesses, the balance sheet is quite brief. It shows what the business owns (its assets) and what it owes (its liabilities). It's very similar to the net worth statement you did earlier. On the next page is an example.

We only show one year, but you should examine three years' worth of statements to note changes in assets, liabilities, and net worth. Pay close attention to the assets, however, because that's what you're buying. If the seller is asking you to pay more than what the assets are worth, that "extra" is called goodwill, going concern value, or blue sky, which we'll discuss in the next chapter. For now, let's concentrate on the assets.

Theoretically, if the business owner sells all the assets and pays off all the liabilities, he or she is left with the net worth (in cash). But many times the assets aren't worth what's stated on the balance sheet. Look at the $72,000 inventory item on Casual Fashions' sheet. Is that what the inventory's really worth? Maybe, maybe not. Suppose it's $72,000 worth of last year's fashions. Or $72,000 worth of mood rings. Similarly, the $33,700 accounts receivable may consist of a large percentage of uncollectable accounts. The fixed assets, shown as having a book value of $27,000, may also be worth more or less than that amount.

It's important to realize that what you're buying is usually the inventory and the fixed assets. Both need to be valued in terms of their *present worth,* not what the balance sheet says they're worth. You may need to bring in an outside appraiser, or call a used equipment dealer to help you make these evaluations.

As far as supporting information is concerned, you need lists of what the assets include, and the inventory amount on the balance sheet must tally with the actual physical items. A list of fixed assets like cash registers, shelves, and deep-fat fryers should show their original cost, any depreciation taken, and the present book value.

For example, let's assume a business shows a walk-in freezer purchased seven years ago for $15,000, which is now fully depreciated as an asset. Its book value is zero, but is that what it's worth? Probably not. How can you determine its present value? Call the company that sold the freezer or one specializing in the sale of used restaurant equipment and find out.

BALANCE SHEET
Casual Fashions, Inc.
as of June 30, 19xx

Assets		Liabilities	
Current Assets		Current Liabilities	
Cash	$ 4,200	Notes Payable	$ 8,500
Accounts Receivable	33,700	Current Portion, LTD	9,100
Inventory	72,000	Accounts Payable	29,000
Other C/A	9,100	Accrued Expenses	3,700
		Other Payables	1,300
Total Current Assets	$119,000	Total Current Liabilities	$51,600
Fixed Assets		Long-Term Debt	61,000
(net of depreciation)	27,000	Total Liabilities	$112,600
Other Assets	8,200		
		NET WORTH	
		Owner's Equity	$ 33,000
		Retained Earnings	8,600
		Total Net Worth	$ 41,600
TOTAL ASSETS	$154,200	LIABILITIES + NET WORTH	$154,200

THE INCOME STATEMENT

The income statement (sometimes called the "P & L" for profit and loss) shows what the business took in from sales and what its expenses were from an *accounting* standpoint. Unless it's called a cash flow statement it doesn't totally reflect the actual income and expenses of the business. Here are the major points to be aware of when reading an income statement:

1. Cash taken in from sources other than sales—like the proceeds of a loan or an investment the owner makes—don't show on the income statement.
2. If the business is repaying a loan, only the interest portion of the loan shows on the income statement.

The principal is a real (cash) expense but not an accounting (tax) expense.

3. Income statements often show deductions for depreciation. This isn't a real expense; no one has written a check to "Depreciation." Depreciation results from spreading the cost of an asset (delivery van, computer) over a number of years as dictated by the latest IRS guidelines.

With these diffferences in mind, let's look at three years of income statements for Harry's Hardware, Inc. There are a number of things you want to examine carefully:

- growth
- profits
- owner's compensation
- expenses.

Growth

Most business analysts use the dollar amount of sales as an indicator of growth. There's absolutely nothing wrong with this as long as you realize there are two kinds of growth in a business—inflated and real. For example, suppose a business does $200,000 in sales for one year. At the beginning of the next year the owner raises prices 10 percent and keeps them at that new level all year, and dollar sales in this second year are $220,000. Was there any growth? There was inflated growth—the 10 percent gain on $200,000, or $20,000, to produce the total of $220,000. However, there was no real growth; the business didn't sell any additional *volume*.

Let's suppose the same conditions exist (that is, a 10 percent price increase) but sales are $240,000. That's a $40,000 increase, or 20 percent, over the previous year. Since 10 percent went into price increases, the other 10 percent (the real growth) came from more sales, not just the same amount of sales at a higher price.

Very often the inflation rate is used by analysts as the baseline for real growth. If a business grows 15 percent from one year to the next (in dollar sales) and the inflation rate is 8 percent, analysts say the business grew at 7 percent.

COMPARATIVE INCOME STATEMENTS
Harry's Hardware, Inc.

	19x1	19x2	19x3
Sales	$215,000	$260,000	$272,000
Cost of Sales	130,000	180,000	168,000
Gross Profit	$ 85,000	$ 80,000	$104,000
Expenses			
Employee wages	12,000	15,000	16,500
Payroll taxes & expenses	8,000	9,500	10,200
Business supplies	1,000	1,000	1,400
Repairs & maintenance	400	1,800	900
Advertising	3,700	4,200	3,900
Car, delivery, travel	2,500	2,200	3,500
Accounting & legal	800	1,700	1,200
Rent	10,000	10,000	13,000
Telephone	2,000	2,900	3,000
Utilities	1,800	1,900	2,000
Insurance	2,100	2,700	2,900
Taxes	600	700	800
Interest	4,000	5,000	4,100
Depreciation	3,000	3,900	3,500
Owner's salary	18,500	22,700	25,000
Miscellaneous	2,000	2,100	3,200
Total expenses	72,400	87,300	95,100
Profit (loss) before tax	$ 12,600	($ 7,300)	$ 8,900
Federal and state taxes	2,500	—	300
Profit (loss) after tax	$ 10,100	($ 7,300)	$ 8,600

Just because a business hasn't been growing isn't an indication you should discard it. However, you should determine the reason for any lack of growth. Often it's simply because the present owner is content with his or her work schedule and salary and no longer pushes for growth. However, a business that declines over several years—one having fewer sales each year—may not be salvageable.

In the case of Harry's Hardware, the total percent growth from 19x1 to 19x2 was

$$\frac{\$260{,}000 - \$215{,}000}{\$215{,}000} \times 100 = 21\%$$

If inflation during 19x2 was 10 percent, then Harry's experienced real growth is 11 percent, which is quite commendable. For 19x2 to 19x3, the total growth was

$$\frac{\$272{,}000 - \$260{,}000}{\$260{,}000} \times 100 = 4.6\%$$

Now suppose inflation was 10 percent again. Then Harry's didn't grow; it declined by 5.4 percent, or 10 percent minus 4.6 percent.

Very often, changes from one year to the other aren't as important as the long-term trend. What is Harry's average growth over the two years?

$$\frac{11\% - 5.4\%}{2} = 2.8\%$$

Notice the minus sign signifying negative growth or decline. A business that keeps pace with inflation or grows is a worthwhile prospect; but beware of the one whose rate of growth is less than the rate of inflation.

Profits

There are actually three kinds of profits to examine—gross profit, profit before tax, and profit after tax. Let's start with gross profit, which may also be called gross margin or operating profit. In most small businesses except manufacturing, the gross profit is computed by subtracting the cost of the goods sold (called Cost of Sales in our example) from the sales. The lower the gross profit, the less cash available to cover the fixed expenses like rent and utilities. Remember, fixed expenses must be paid even if no business is done.

It's possible to get average values for gross profit for various kinds of businesses simply by calling a banker or checking business reference books at the library. The average value or gross profit for hardware stores over the years has been 33 percent. Let's see what Harry's looks like.

$$\text{19x1: } \frac{\$85{,}000}{\$215{,}000} \times 100 = 39.5\%$$

$$\text{19x2: } \frac{\$80{,}000}{\$260{,}000} \times 100 = 30.8\%$$

$$\text{19x3: } \frac{\$104{,}000}{\$272{,}000} \times 100 = 38.2\%$$

3-year average: 36.2%

What happened in 19x2? Maybe he paid too much for his goods or failed to raise his prices when his hardware distributors raised theirs. There may be a number of explanations, and it's important you find out what they are.

Profits before and after tax aren't as important in small business as large ones, but they should be examined. Harry may have wiped out the pre-tax profit of $12,600 in 19x1 simply by paying himself that much more. Of course, that would increase Harry's salary from $18,500 to $31,100 and put him in a much higher personal tax bracket. It's more likely Harry's accountant had him report a taxable personal income of $18,500 and a taxable business profit of $12,600 to keep the overall tax bill to a minimum.

Pre-tax profit margins for hardware stores have run 2.5 to 4.0 percent in the past. For Harry's, we have values of

19x1: 5.9%
19x2: (2.8%)
19x3: 3.3%
3-year average: 2.1 percent

Numbers in parentheses are negative values; that is, the 19x2 profit margin was −2.8 percent.

Owner's Compensation

One of the critical elements in a business purchase is how much you can expect to pay yourself. In two earlier exercises you (1) specified the amount you need to live on, and (2) estimated your personal monthly expenses. It makes little sense to get into a business where you suffer financially. Don't believe you can happily live in poverty to have your own business; it just doesn't work. People rarely change their lifestyle drastically when they become business owners.

Let's look at our friend Harry. For the year 19x3, his salary was $25,000. Does that mean you can count on that as a minimum if you buy Harry's business?

The answer is maybe, because it depends on a number of things. Suppose you must borrow from Harry or a bank in order to buy the business, and the payment is higher than Harry had. That's going to cut into available cash. Your business plan will tell you how that higher payment will affect your salary.

Looking at the owner's salary as an expense to the business, we see it represents the following percentages to sales:

19x1:	8.6%
19x2:	8.7%
19x3:	9.2%

It's been increasing and may be reaching its limits. The average value of owner's salary for hardware stores is 5 percent of sales.

One other thing to keep in mind is that often the owner's salary isn't comparable to salary from an employer because there are a number of *legal* tax benefits that come from business ownership that simply aren't available to a wage earner. For example, the business may provide a car and housing.

Expenses

Examine other expenses (supplies, advertising, telephone) to see if any look strange or bring up questions in your mind. As the sales increase, expenses usually increase as well, but look for any that are rising very rapidly.

Check any large items against industry averages. Hardware stores pay around 2.5 percent of sales for rent. Harry's figures show

19x1:	4.7%
19x2:	3.8%
19x3:	4.8%

Why are Harry' figures so high? What does his rent include?

Also be alert to those items having very low or nonexistent values. If you're looking at a business with a good deal of older equipment, you expect to see expenses for maintenance. If it's not there, you may get saddled with it later. Also, if the business shows no cost for advertising, this may mean the owner's done little to develop new markets.

SUMMARY

When you do the analysis, you get a fair idea of the strengths and weaknesses of a business. If any of the critical values (growth, profit, owner's compensation or expenses) seem too low or too high, find out why. Sure, numbers don't tell the whole story, and national averages may not hold for small businesses in Smalltown, Minnesota. However, this is the time to find out. It's one thing to buy a Smalltown business and discover it has higher than average profits; it's quite another to realize its heating costs eat up most of those profits. If the business isn't for you, now is the time to politely remove yourself from any future negotiation. If you're dealing with a broker, go over your reasons for turning the business down so he or she can become more attuned to what you're looking for. You may not want to be quite so candid if you're working directly with the seller; business owners see their businesses in personal terms, and a criticism may be viewed as an insult.

We see cases where a buyer finds a number of weaknesses in a business, presents these findings to the seller, and is countered with that frequently-used phrase, "Yeah, but the business has great potential." It may, but you should never pay for it.

That brings us to the next chapter: how to determine price and how to negotiate with the seller.

Chapter SEVEN

Negotiations with the Seller

In this chapter we're going to discuss how to establish price and terms with the seller. We're assuming the seller is providing financing over and above the down payment. If the seller doesn't provide financing, and you can't pay the full price in cash, you'll need outside financing—friends, relatives, a commercial bank (with or without SBA participation), a commercial lending company, or investors. Chapter Nine will show you how to do this. Normally the seller of a small business provides all or a major portion of the financing.

Before we get into the mechanics of determining price and terms, let's review some basic information about sellers.

WHERE YOU ARE NOW

In some cases the seller may be willing to supply all the business information you need to evaluate the asking price and terms up front. Other sellers may be reluctant to give you enough financial and lease data to see if you and the seller can agree on a price. Any agreement you reach with the seller must be subject to your approval of the books, records, lease, and anything else you need to make a final decision.

The question often comes up with first-timers: Do I make an offer or see the books first? The answer should be obvious, but let's look at the seller's point of view for a moment. Sellers' reluctance to show books and records probably results from the belief that you may not be a serious buyer. You may not be the first prospect, and sellers can grow tired of the "tire kickers." After all, they don't want to show their financial records to just any casual observer. As strange as it may sound, sellers may see you as a competitor or, worse yet, the IRS itself.

As we said before, many sellers want to test your seriousness by insisting you make a written offer accompanied by a deposit before they show you their records, and also before you meet the landlord; they want to see the "color of your money" before revealing all the information about their business. They may also want to see if the two of you can get together on price before they spend the time digging up everything you want to know about the business.

Brokers see so many cases of idle curiosity among buyers that they also prefer buyer and seller to set a price before books, records and leases are viewed. Too many sellers and brokers feel too much time is wasted showing financial data only to discover the buyer really can't afford the place. By completing your net worth statement (Chapter Four) you save yourself from this embarrassment.

If you try to get financial records and other data and the seller or broker tells you to make an offer first, and you're very interested, here's what to do. Make an offer, but put a sentence in your offer or proposal stating your deal is subject to, and contingent upon, your approval of the seller's books and records. This little sentence protects you in case the books and records don't support what the seller tells you.

WHAT DETERMINES PRICE?

Some words on price: there is no *right* price. A business is only worth what someone is willing to pay for it. A junkyard in Hoboken, New Jersey doesn't have the same appeal as a fine inn in Vermont, even though the owner's salary and profit may be the same.

A business is made up of the following: (1) tangible assets such as equipment, the value of the lease, leasehold improvements (these are improvements that the seller of the business makes to the real property), the inventory, and (2) intangible assets: the name of the business, its trade secrets, patents, copyrights, recipes, reputation—which are also called goodwill. Goodwill simply reflects the reasonable expectation of future profits.

The equipment in a business is much like an automobile. It has a high initial price when new, but the minute it's used, the price declines. In most small businesses the equipment is only worth the amount of income it can produce. Outdated or outmoded equipment can actually be a negative factor; it can cost more to maintain or repair it than the income it produces.

Inventory is a real figure determined on a wholesale price when the business changes hands. In other words, if the seller pays $10,000 for the inventory, that's what you pay as long as the inventory is saleable. There may be some exceptions to this, such as rare wine, antiques, or other commodities that increase in price with age.

The lease and leasehold may also have value. In some businesses, the real estate may be available as well as the business. We suggest you use your cash to buy assets rather than goodwill. If cash is no problem and the real estate is available, then you might consider buying it. However, keep in mind that if you decide to sell, you may end up being a landlord if the next owner only wants to buy the business. Make sure owning and operating a small business is for you before you invest in the real property. If the seller wants to sell the property, see if you can get him or her to give you an option to purchase it at a specific price *after* you've owned the business a while.

Some experts say you can't buy goodwill, and in a sense they're right; the buyer becomes the new goodwill. Our feeling is that there is goodwill value if a reasonably competent person can buy the business and do at least as well as the present owner. Any seller wants and expects goodwill to be part of the selling price.

PRICING BUSINESSES

Pricing a business establishes its value. Until a knowledgeable buyer and a willing seller agree on price, it can be said that the business has no value or, at best, the value is academic. If you do any research into business values, you run across such terms as asset value, book value, formula value, stock value, times-earnings value; the list is long and frustrating. We're going to give you a simpler method to determine value. It's not foolproof, but it is logical and enables you and a seller to evaluate and negotiate specific *parts* of the price rather than simply trying to argue over the total.

When you buy a house, you buy an asset. Although most people don't do it, you could hire an independent real estate appraiser to value the property. These appraisers generally give a minimum of two different values: (1) the replacement cost, and (2) a value based on the recent sale of comparable properties in the neighborhood.

When you buy a business, you buy assets, but you also buy something else. In one sense you buy an investment; you put money into something (a business) that will return money to you (a salary and, hopefully, some profit). So we can say the total value of a business is equal to the asset value plus the business value. Some experts speak of these two elements as tangible asset value and intangible asset value. The term tangible assets refers to those items that can be seen and touched—inventory, equipment, land and buildings, vehicles, furniture. The intangible assets like location, an established name, trained employees, reputation, and reliable suppliers all contribute to the ability of a small business to make sales, pay expenses, provide a salary for the owner, repay loans, purchase tangible assets, and make a profit. The term *goodwill* is used to describe the value of intangible assets, and most accountants will tell you not to pay for goodwill. However, most sellers feel goodwill does have value.

We're proposing a step-wise approach for calculating the price, or *market value* of a business and wish to thank James Howard, founder of Country Business Services, for the basic theory. We'll use the following steps:

1. Determine the asset value; that is, what to pay for the assets.
2. Calculate the business value:
   a. Construct a "normalized" income statement.
   b. Determine the owner's salary and profit before tax.
   c. Apply standard percentages to salary to determine the "excess earnings" of the business, if any. Add this to profits, if any.
   d. Rate the business in eight categories, creating a factor which, when multiplied by the excess earnings, gives the business value.
3. Add asset value to business value to determine market value.

ASSET VALUE

As we said before, you must determine what the assets are worth to you. The seller may put an arbitrary price on assets based on either their original or replacement cost, both of which probably exceed current market value. We say "probably" because some assets like land and buildings may increase in value, but most tend to decrease in value over time.

There's a form (ASSET VALUE) below to record the assets you're buying, along with their historical costs and market values. Use Item 1(b) to record other current assets* besides inventory. What might these be? The seller may include accounts receivable or prepaid expenses like rent or insurance

* Current Assets are defined as those whose life within the business is one year or less.

ASSET VALUE OF ______________________

	Historical Cost	Market Value	Notes
1. Current Assets			
a. Inventory	$	$	
b. Other (specify):			
2. Fixed Assets			
a. Land			
b. Buildings			
c. Equipment:			
(1)			
(2)			
(3)			
(4)			
(5)			
(6)			
d. Furniture			
e. Fixtures			
f. Vehicles			
g. Other (specify):			
3. Other Assets:			
a.			
b.			
c.			
TOTALS	$	$	

ASSET VALUE of Small Grocery Store, Inc.

	Historical Cost	Market Value	Notes
1. Current Assets			
a. Inventory	$20,000	$18,000	10% of inventory is obsolete.
b. Other (specify):			
Tax deposit	500	500	Will revert to buyer in one year.
2. Fixed Assets			
a. Land	—	—	
b. Buildings	—	—	
c. Equipment:			
(1) 3 coolers	10,100	3,700	
(2) meat chest	5,200	2,000	Estimates from Ace
(3) freezer	2,100	1,000	Used Equipment Co.
(4) dairy chest	2,400	1,000	
(5) cash register	2,300	1,000	According to NCR Corp.
(6)			
d. Furniture	3,000	1,000	Over 8 years old.
e. Fixtures	12,000	8,000	Shelves need painting.
f. Vehicles	11,000	5,000	3-year old van. Value according to NADA.
g. Other (specify):			
1 Outdoor sign	2,000	1,000	Agreed to by seller.
3. Other Assets:			
a.			
b.			
c.			
TOTALS	$70,600	$42,200	

that have value to you. Item 3, Other Assets, is used to list items that don't fit under current or fixed assets. For example, an existing contract would have value if you bought the business. Let's look at the grocery store analysis above. Notice that each item in the list is examined and a market value established either by an outside source (Ace Used Equipment Co., NCR Corp., NADA) or by negotiation and agreement with the seller. Remember, we want market value, not historical value, book value, or replacement value; we want to know what these specific assets are worth right now.

BUSINESS VALUE

Coming up with the market price of the business portion of a business has always been fraught with problems. Some people like formulas. Some experts say the selling price for many small retail establishments is three to four times their monthly gross. An accounting firm or advertising agency may be priced at 1½ to 3 times annual billings; but who's to say how many "times"? Some people perform long and involved return-on-investment calculations. Other folks claim a business should never sell for less than book value. And on it goes. As we said, our method certainly isn't foolproof, but it is repeatable and logical. It gives you a *general* indication of the value of the going concern—the business value, or goodwill.

The first thing we must do is normalize the income statement. We're not going to distort it—merely remove or adjust any abnormalities. Sound confusing? Let's look at some examples. One hospitality business we saw listed six antique cars and their upkeep in the financial information, but the cars weren't being sold with the business. Therefore, their cost and upkeep had to be removed from the income statement. Another business didn't spend anything for equipment maintenance for two years, and now these assets are badly in need of repairs. The cost of these future repairs must be added to the income statement. The third business had the entire family on the payroll even though the kids really didn't work there.

Sit down with income statements from one or two years and examine each item to determine if it should be adjusted or normalized. Let's look at an income statement for Small Grocery Store, Inc.:

Net Sales	$150,000
Cost of Sales	95,000
Gross Profit	$ 55,000
Expenses:	
Employee wages	$ 15,000
Payroll taxes	7,000
Supplies	500
Advertising	300
Travel	2,000
Rent & Utilities	6,000
Maintenance	400
Insurance	300
Interest	2,000
Depreciation	1,000
Owner's salary	16,000
Miscellaneous	400
Total Expenses	50,900
Profit (Loss) Before Tax	$ 4,100

Now let's see what our imaginary buyer discovers about the expense items.

Item	Findings	Adjustment
Employee wages	$5,000 paid to seller's teenage daughter, who doesn't work in the business.	Reduce by $5,000 to $10,000.
Payroll taxes	Because this item is 22.5 percent of all wages plus owner's salary, it must be reduced by 22.5 percent of $5,000.	Reduce by $1,100 to $5,900.
Supplies	O.K.	None.
Advertising	Small food stores spend an average of 1 percent of sales on advertising. Increase to 1 percent of $150,000 or $1,500.	Increase to $1,500.
Travel	Owner took family on trip costing $1,000 and charged as business expense.	Reduce by $1,000 to $1,000.
Rent & Utilities	A 10 percent increase is expected for the next year.	Increase by $600 to $6,600.
Maintenance	Too low. Average annual expense should be $800.	Increase to $800.
Insurance	Business badly under-insured. Need $1,000 additional premium.	Increase by $1,000 to $1,300.
Interest	Will assume seller's note.	None.
Depreciation	O.K.	None.
Owner's salary	Too low for new owner.	Increase by $2,000 to $18,000.
Miscellaneous	O.K.	None.

The normalized income statement looks like this:

Net Sales	$150,000
Cost of Sales	95,000
Gross Profit	$ 55,000

Expenses:	
Employee wages	$ 10,000
Payroll taxes	5,900
Supplies	500
Advertising	1,500
Travel	1,000
Rent & Utilities	6,600
Maintenance	800
Insurance	1,300
Interest	2,000
Depreciation	1,000
Owner's salary	18,000
Miscellaneous	400
Total Expenses	49,000
Profit (Loss) Before Tax	$ 6,000

When we normalize the income statement, we simultaneously complete the second step (determining the owner's salary and profit before tax). The owner's salary is $18,000 and the profit before tax $6,000. We call this combined figure, $24,000, the total return on investment to the buyer, what the business earns after everything else is taken care of.

In the next two steps we want to discover what the "excess earnings" of the business are. Excess earnings are those earnings beyond what you would expect of the *average* business of this kind in an *average* location. The theory behind excess earnings is this: if the business provides only an average owner's salary and no profit, then buying the business provides no real business value to the buyer. He or she could get a job running the business and earn the same salary. No one buys or pays for a job and a business buyer shouldn't either. It's the something extra, the *excess* earnings, that have value. To determine whether or not the business provides excess earnings, we need to know if an $18,000 salary is normal or average. Our banker tells us the salaries of small grocery store owners average 9.5 percent of net sales. So our normal is

$$9.5\% \times \$150{,}000 = \$14{,}250$$

and the excess earnings are the difference between that average amount and our salary, or

$$\$18{,}000 - \$14{,}250 = \$3{,}750$$

If our banker told us the average owner's salary was 15 percent of sales, the normal salary would be $22,500, which is greater than the projected level of $18,000, and there are *no* excess earnings. This is important; excess earnings are either there or they aren't; there are no such things as *negative* earnings.

Now we add excess earnings to profits. In our example, we have

Excess earnings	$3,750
Profit	6,000
Return	$9,750

We call the total of excess earnings and profit *return;* it's what's returned to the owner over and above a normal compensation for managing the business.

So our buyer of Small Grocery Store, Inc. can expect an annual return of $9,750. What's that worth? The entire amount? More than that? Less? Most business analysts estimate the annual return is worth anywhere from one to five times its calculated value. In our example that means the annual return could have a business value from $9,750 (one times its value) to five times that amount, or $48,750. That leaves a lot of room for negotiation between a buyer and a seller! Why such a range?

How much annual return is worth depends on a number of factors relating not only to the attractiveness of the business in general, but its performance in the past, its environment, and the buyer's desire to own and operate it. These qualities are hard to evaluate, but giving them a one to five rating system can be helpful. Here are eight different categories in which to rate the business, including five where you must *use your judgment.* Once you rate each category, find the average overall rating for the business. This number times the annual return is the business value.

In the table on the next page is a blank rating form for your use; if you're rating more than one business, simply copy the form. Following the blank form is a rating the potential buyer gives Small Grocery Store, Inc.

BUSINESS RATING FORM

Rating Category	Range of Values	Value Given
1. Number of years the business has been in existence	1 = 2 years or less 2 = 3–4 years 3 = 5–6 years 4 = 7–8 years 5 = 9 years or more	
2. Number of years the seller has owned the business	1 = 2 years or less 2 = 3–4 years 3 = 5–6 years 4 = 7–8 years 5 = 9 years or more	
3. Reason for sale	See Chapter Five. Take your ratings there and make the following change: 1 = rating of 1–2 2 = rating of 3–4 3 = rating of 5–6 4 = rating of 7–8 5 = rating of 9–10	
4. Competition	1 = many competitors, market glutted 2 = above average number 3 = normal competitive situation 4 = below average number 5 = unique market position	
5. Risk	1 = extremely high 2 = high 3 = normal 4 = low 5 = extremely low	
6. Growth of business in the past	1 = rapid decline 2 = below inflation by 5% or more 3 = at the rate of inflation 4 = above inflation by 5–10% 5 = very high growth	
7. Location	1 = location inhibits business 2 = below average 3 = average 4 = desirable 5 = highly desirable	
8. Desirability of business	1 = minimum to none 2 = low 3 = normal 4 = high 5 = very high	

TOTALS OF ABOVE __________

DIVIDE BY 8 (MULTIPLIER) __________

SMALL GROCERY STORE, INC.

Rating Category	Value Used for Our Example	Value Given
1. Number of years the business has been in existence	7½	4
2. Number of years the seller has owned the business	2	1
3. Reason for sale	wants larger business	3
4. Competition	normal	3
5. Risk	high	2
6. Growth of business in the past	7% below inflation	2
7. Location	average	3
8. Desirability of business	low	2
TOTALS OF ABOVE		20
DIVIDE BY 8 (MULTIPLIER)		2.5

Therefore, in our example, the business value (goodwill) is worth 2.5 times the annual return of $9,750 or

2.5 × $9,750 = $24,400 (rounded off)

The total market value of Small Grocery Store, Inc., is the asset value plus the business value:

Asset value	$42,200
Business value	24,400
Market value	$66,600

Our method does break down at the high and low ends. If you rate a business as *all* ones, its business value is really zero and you shouldn't buy it. If a business is *all* fives, its business value might exceed our high of five times the annual return. In some special businesses with unique appeal, the multiplier may go as high as eight, but that's a rare case. We've included a blank form for you to summarize the calculations on your business, and one showing the values for our grocery store.

BUSINESS PRICING FORM

Business: ________

1. Asset Value	$
2. Business Value	
a. Annual Return	$
b. Multiplier	
c. (a) times (b)	$
3. Add (1) and (2c) above to give Market Value	$______

BUSINESS PRICING FORM

Business: Small Grocery Store, Inc.

1. Asset Value	$42,200
2. Business Value	
a. Annual Return	$ 9,750
b. Multiplier	2.5
c. (a) times (b)	$24,400
3. Add (1) and (2c) above to give Market Value	$66,600

Once you do this analysis of the market value of the business, you have a way to go over specific items with the seller, especially the items that constitute that elusive thing called goodwill.

Now let's examine a counterpart of price, the terms.

TERMS

Some deals can get extremely complex, but most small business sales involve a down payment that typically ranges from 20 to 40 percent of the total selling price, with the remainder financed by the seller. Obviously, if the seller is unwilling to provide any or all of the financing, you have to seek OPM—other people's money. The usual source of OPM is a bank loan, which we'll discuss in Chapter Nine. To understand how terms work, let's look at Small Grocery Store, Inc., with its market value of $66,600. We'll assume that buyer and seller agree on a price of $65,000 and must now agree on terms. The first term is the amount of the down payment, which may be influenced by many factors. Too small a down payment may hamper the seller financially. It is hoped that the seller's accountant will have advised the seller of any tax factors before the time of sale.

Let's assume in our example that our buyer comes up with a down payment of $20,000 (about 31 percent of $65,000) and that the seller is willing to finance the balance of $45,000. Now the question becomes how is the $45,000 to be paid to the seller? If it's paid too quickly, the cash drain will undoubtedly cripple the business. Buyer and seller must set up a payment schedule that can be carried by the business but also pay off the seller in a reasonable amount of time.

The most common approach to seller financing is to select an interest rate and a term (in years) that meets the needs of both buyer and seller. You can compare the effects of term and interest rate using the table in Chapter Eight on page 74. Terms from 5 to 15 years (the normal lower and upper limits of business loans) and interest rates from 6 to 20 percent in 2 percent increments are given. If you know the terms and interest rate, you can use the table to determine the monthly payment on $1,000 of borrowed capital.

Let's say our seller wants the $45,000 paid back in six years at 16 percent interest. Looking at the table we see that the montly payment is $21.69 for each $1,000 borrowed. For the full loan, the monthly payment is

$$\$21.69 \times 45 = \$976.05$$

Can the business afford this amount? You really don't know until you do your cash flow projections as part of your business plan (Chapter Eight).

If the business can't carry a monthly payment of $976.05, you must lower the interest rate, lengthen the term, or both. For example, if we keep the interest rate at 16 percent but lengthen the term to 12 years in our example, our monthly payment per $1,000 from the table is $15.66 and the full payment is

$$\$15.66 \times 45 = \$704.70$$

Now let's assume we determine the most the business can afford is $600 per month. Let's also assume that the lowest interest rate the seller will accept is 14 percent. The first step is to divide $600 by 45 to determine what we can afford in monthly payments per $1,000 borrowed:

$$\frac{\$600}{45} = \$13.33$$

Looking again at our table, we see a 15-year term gives a monthly payment of $13.32. Is the seller willing to give a 15-year term to keep his 14 percent? That's something else to negotiate.

Some sellers may talk about variable interest rates. This means you don't have a fixed payment but rather one which varies as a function of some value like the prime interest rate. Another item that may be introduced into the negotiations is called a balloon payment. This means you and the seller negotiate a normal loan but the loan never goes to completion; at a predetermined time, the remaining balance of the loan comes due before the term is exhausted.

Suppose the seller of our grocery store proposes the following: a $45,000 loan at 12 percent for 12 years with a balloon at 7 years. What does this mean? First, let's go to our table and find the monthly payment:

$$\$13.13 \times 45 = \$590.85$$

The buyer makes 84 monthly payments (7 years × 12) of $590.85 for a total of $49,631.40. How much of the principal remains is important because that amount must now be paid to the seller in full. You need a fancy financial calculator or an amortization schedule from a bank to figure this out, but the $49,631.40 paid over 84 months breaks down as follows:

Interest:	$31,226.29
Principal:	$18,405.11
	$49,631.40

The remaining balance of the loan is

$45,000.00
−18,405.11
$26,594.89

and is fully due and payable to the seller in the 85th month. The normal process is to finance this amount with a bank. In some instances the remaining balance can again be negotiated with the seller, setting a new interest rate and term.

Now let's discuss some of the mechanics of negotiations.

FINAL NEGOTIATIONS

You can only base your initial offer on what the seller is asking and the price you determined using the method we supplied. Don't forget, the broker represents the seller and should not be telling you what to offer. Nor should you put the broker in an embarrassing position by asking for his or her advice. The broker is duty-bound to try to get the best possible price for the seller.

Below is an offer to purchase, which we suggest you present to the seller. It both protects you and demonstrates your seriousness to the seller.

If a broker is involved in the sale, he or she will have buyer and seller execute a purchase and sale agreement; there is a sample following the offer to purchase.

OFFER TO PURCHASE

I offer to purchase assets and goodwill of the business known as ______________________________, located at______________________________.

The full purchase price shall be $______________ (including inventory).

The full down payment shall be $______________ (including inventory).

I will assume existing encumbrances of approximately $__________, payable at $__________ per month, which includes ______ percent interest.
The balance of approximately $__________ will be paid to the seller at $__________ per month *or more* including ______ percent interest per annum.*

All equipment must be in good working order and the seller agrees to train the buyer without cost for two weeks. This sale is subject to the buyer's approval of the seller's books and records, lease, and the landlord's approval of said lease.

This sale shall close on ______(date)______, and possession to be given at the same time.

This sale shall comply with the state bulk sales provision of the Uniform Commercial Code (UCC).

______________________________ ______________________

SIGNATURE DATE

Attached is a deposit for $______________. This check shall not be cashed until the terms of this agreement have been met and shall be subtracted from the down payment. If this offer is not accepted by ______(date)______, or buyer does not approve the books, records, or lease, or contingent financing is not secured, this deposit check shall be returned.

*NOTE: "or more" means that you can pay the balance of the loan to the seller without any prepayment penalty. You might also want to check the existing encumberances to see if they allow for an "or more" clause or if they require some form of prepayment penalty. Remember, the down payment, any existing encumberances you are assuming, and the money owed the seller should add up to the full purchase price.

If the seller is not providing all the financing, you need to add a contingent financing clause—"This offer is contingent upon the buyer's securing proper outside financing."

PURCHASE AND SALE AGREEMENT

Date ___/___/___

1. The Buyer agrees to purchase from the Seller the business described as follows, including all equipment, fixtures, goodwill, inventory, trademarks, trade names and leasehold rights. This business is known as: ______________________________

______________________________, a (corporation) (partnership) (proprietorship) ______

located at: ______________________________

2. The purchase price of $______________ shall be paid as follows:

a.	$______________	Deposit on the date of this agreement included in down payment.
b.	______________	Additional deposit upon acceptance by Seller included in down payment.
c.	______________	Balance of down payment due at the closing in cash or certified check.
	$______________	Total Down Payment
d.	______________	Assumption of existing obligation payable as follows: $______ per month (including ______ % interest).
e.	______________	Assumption of existing obligation payable as follows: $______ per month (including ______ % interest).
f.	______________	Balance to Seller payable as follows: $__________ or more per month (including ______ % interest).
g.	______________	Additional terms: ______________________________
	$______________	Total Purchase Price

____

____

____

3. The closing shall take place at __________ o'clock ☐ A.M. ☐ P.M. on ______________, 19____, at the office of ______________ ______________________________; closing costs shall be shared equally by Buyer and Seller.

4. The full purchase price shall include inventory of $__________ at Sellers cost. If the actual amount is more or less, the purchase price and down payment shall be adusted accordingly.

- ☐ However in no event shall the inventory amount exceed $______________.
- ☐ At Sellers cost and paid direct to Seller in addition to purchase price.
- ☐ ______________________________

5. The sales tax on fixtures and equipment, if any, shall be paid for by the Buyer.

6. Seller warrants that at the time physical possession is delivered to Buyer, all equipment will be in working order and that the premises will pass all inspections necessary to conduct such business.

7. The Buyer and Seller agree to execute all documents necessary to consummate this transaction including where applicable, such documents as are necessary to comply with the Bulk Transfer provisions of the Uniform Commercial Code.

8. All deposits shall be held by Broker who, at its option, may hold Buyer's deposit check in an uncashed form until this agreement has been signed by the Seller.

9. This document contains the entire understanding of the parties and there are no oral agreements, understandings or representations relied upon by the parties. Any modifications must be in writing and signed by all parties.

10. The Seller warrants that it has a clear and marketable title to the business being sold except as mentioned above.

11. Seller shall deliver to Buyer a valid lease or assignment of lease for a period of ______ years, at a rental of $__________ per month. Option of ______________________________

12. The following adjustments and prorations shall be made at closing, rent, security deposits, __________, __________, __________, __________, __________, __________ and __________.

13. In case any litigation is instituted to collect any sum due Broker, the Buyer and Seller, jointly and severally, agree to pay the expenses incurred by the Broker in connection with such suit, including attorney's fees.

14. If the seller fails to accept this agreement by midnight ______________, 19____, then the Buyer may revoke this agreement.

PURCHASER AND SELLER INDIVIDUALLY ACKNOWLEDGE RECEIPT OF A COPY OF THIS AGREEMENT.

THIS IS A LEGALLY BINDING DOCUMENT. READ IT CAREFULLY. IF YOU DO NOT UNDERSTAND IT, CONSULT AN ATTORNEY. BROKER IS NOT AUTHORIZED TO GIVE LEGAL ADVICE.

PURCHASER hereby agrees to buy on the terms set forth above.

Dated: ______________________________

PURCHASER: ______________________________

____

Address ______________________________

City ______________ State ______ Zip ______

Telephone: ( ) ______________________________

______________________________ Broker

The Seller agrees to sell on the terms set forth above.

Dated: ______________________________

BUSINESS NAME ______________________________

SELLER: ______________________________

____

Address ______________________________

City ______________ State ______ Zip ______

Telephone ( ) ______________________________

Once you complete the offer to purchase, you're ready to meet with the seller. Tell the seller you have given his or her business a lot of thought, you're interested, and want to present an offer. Don't get too anxious. Say you tried to take everything into account including what you know about the business and your own situation. You're going to need some money to fix the parking lot or paint the sign. Present your offer and keep quiet. Don't be concerned about any initial reaction. Sellers may yell, scream, cry, rant, and rave about how they can't possibly accept the offer. When they calm down enough for you to ask what the problem is, you may find it's a minor one.

Address each objection as it occurs. If the problem is the full price or the down payment, say that's all you feel it's worth or all you can swing at this time. If you haven't been given any meaningful numbers yet, tell the owner you had to base the price and terms on what little information he or she did supply. Tell the owner you don't really think the business is worth a higher price or that you need all the cash possible to fix the place up, if the down payment is in question.

Most sellers are concerned about price, the down payment, or terms unless you put in some strange requests like asking the seller to stay and work free for a year. Handle each objection or counterproposal objectively, but don't commit yourself. Just listen. When the seller is done telling you why the offer is unacceptable, suggest taking a few days to think about it some more.

Sometimes the seller will respond to your offer with a price that's acceptable to you. When that occurs, make the necessary corrections on the offer to purchase form, being sure all the numbers add up properly. Both you and the seller sign the agreement and initial all changes. Be sure all changes are made on all copies, and that the seller receives a copy.

If the seller refuses your offer, tell the seller that the proposal is the best you can do. Pick up the offer to purchase form and walk slowly toward the door, being sure to thank the seller for his or her time. The seller may call you back before you leave. If not, head for home. However, make sure you leave your home telephone number in case the seller has a change of heart and decides to accept your offer.

There's not much else you can do if the seller doesn't accept your original proposal and you don't accept any counter-proposals. In order for the sale to take place, something has to give. Either the seller or you—or both. If after a few days you still want the business, give the seller a call and say you're still interested, and set up another time to get together to reconsider your offer. The seller might have other prospects, so don't wait for him or her to call you if you really want the place.

On the other hand, don't let sellers threaten you with other buyers who are "just as interested as you." There may very well be other buyers; in fact, you should be concerned if you are the *only* one who thinks the business is a good one. But don't let sellers or brokers push you into deals you're not comfortable with even if it means starting your search over again.

Remember, there's no exact formula for pricing a business, no matter how much information you have. Each business is unique and so different from any other that determining the exact price, value, or worth of a business is impossible. We gave you a technique for placing a market value on a business, but the actual sale price is determined by you and the seller.

Also keep in mind that it's rough to cut *both* the asking price and the down payment dramatically, unless the business is obviously overpriced. If you're short of cash, let the seller have his way on the full price and aim for a lower down payment. On the other hand, if cash is no problem and you can meet or exceed the desired down payment, you might want to negotiate the full price. It's hard to say which is a seller's biggest "hot button." Some will refuse to negotiate the full price, and others the down payment. As we said before, much depends on the seller's reason for selling. Retiring sellers are usually more concerned about getting the full price and payment. Those buying another business usually want as much cash (i.e., as big a down payment) as possible.

One final word of caution: when it's over, when you and the seller agree on price and terms, and it looks like you've bought a business—go to the store, buy some candies and place them under your pillow before you go to bed. About 3:00 a.m., when you awake in a total panic and ask yourself "What have I done?" take out the candies and eat them slowly until the panic goes away. Buyer's remorse is natural. In all major decisions we always ask ourselves whether or not we did the right thing. Relax, go back to sleep—you made the right decision.

Chapter EIGHT

The Business Plan

WHY DO A BUSINESS PLAN?

Lawyers use a phrase—*due diligence*—that refers to those things they expect a competent lawyer to know and do. Preparing a business plan is part of the due diligence of operating your own business. You don't have to do one, but you greatly increase your probability of success if you do.

The first reason to prepare a business plan is to secure proper financing if you need it. If you present a business plan to a commercial banker or a private investor, you increase your chances of getting your money. If the seller provides your financing, you don't need a plan for that purpose, but that doesn't mean you don't need a plan. Never commit yourself to the purchase of a business until you feel that the business can survive and pay you a salary.

For example, suppose you buy a business that has no outstanding loans (debts). Because you don't have enough cash to buy the business outright, you take a loan from the seller which you agree to repay at the rate of $1,000 a month. If your business grosses $10,000 a month, that $1,000 loan payment comes right off the top, reducing the amount of available cash. That $1,000 may be too large a financial burden for the business to survive, whereas a $500 payment might permit repayment and growth. A business plan can give these answers.

In general there are four reasons for doing a business plan:

It reduces risk. Remember, good business owners are not dice-throwers. They don't take outrageous risks. By preparing a plan, you reduce your risk because you work things out in advance. Naturally you won't be able to foresee everything that might happen in the future, but you can work through the major events.

It eliminates surprises. The small business world is a highly technical and complex one, and the days of the simple Mom 'n Pop operations over. Running a business without a plan is like driving a car without paying attention to either the rules of the road or where you're going. There's an old saw that says if you have no destination, then any road will take you there. We add, if you have no destination, you'll never know when you get there, either. People who run businesses without plans very often see themselves as victims—victims of the economy, competition, the government, their customers, the bank. They are.

It establishes your method for doing things. Successful businesses today are run according to method. Once you complete your first business plan, you establish an important part of your business method. Like so many things, planning is a learning experience, and you get better at it as time goes by. Your first business plan probably won't be your last, and each one will be easier and better than the one before.

It sets up financing. The business plan establishes in advance how much money you need. It gives your financing sources some reasonable assumptions to examine to see why you're asking for the money and how you plan to pay it back (in the case of a loan) or what return an investor will realize (in the case of equity funds).

THE LOGIC OF PLANNING

Many people don't realize there is a logical system behind a business plan. It looks like this:

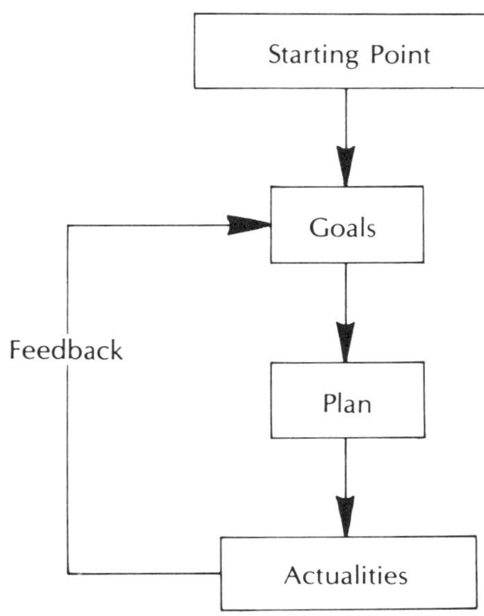

Your starting point is where you are *right now*. It's *not* where you think you should be. It consists of your present skills and everything else you have to work with. The goals are where you want to go: the products or services you will offer, what your sales and profits will be, how much money you want to raise. The plan is the vehicle to help you reach those goals. Actualities are events occurring in the future; they either occcur the way you planned them or they don't. If they don't, you use what you learn to adjust the goals; then there's a new plan, and so on: plan and adjust, plan and adjust.

BUSINESS PLAN MECHANICS

We've included a business plan workbook so you can follow our explanation and then prepare your own plan. Once you complete the plan, have it typed in an attractive, professional format before you present it to others. Yes, neatness does count.

One thing to be aware of right off the bat is that there's no such thing as *the* format for a business plan. This is only a suggested format; if other items occur to you, by all means include them. However, don't add material just to make the plan look bigger; the pros will spot it.

One last word of advice: *You* do the plan. Don't have a consultant or other advisor do it for you, because then it becomes their plan and not yours. We're not against your getting help or having someone check over your material. As a matter of fact, it's a good idea to work on the financial section with the aid of your accountant; but remember, it's your plan and your business.

BUSINESS PLAN—OUTLINE

We'll follow this outline in our discussion and the workbook:

Title page
Summary and Purpose (optional)
Table of Contents

I. The Business
  A. Business Description
    1. Name
    2. Location
    3. Physical facilities
    4. Business history
  B. Products or Services
    1. Description of product line
    2. Proprietary considerations

- C. Management Plan
    1. Organizational form and structure
    2. Résumés of key people
    3. Staffing plan
    4. Supporting services
- D. Operations Plan
    1. Facilities and equipment
    2. Plans for growth and expansion
    3. Overall schedule
    4. Process description
- E. Risks (optional)

II. Marketing Plan
- A. Marketing Research
    1. Description of market
    2. Industry trends
    3. Target market
    4. Competition
- B. Objectives and strategy
- C. Pricing Policy
- D. Sales Terms
- E. Method of Sales and Distribution
- F. Customer Service
- G. Advertising and Promotion
- H. Forecasts

III. Financial Data
- A. Proposal
- B. Source and Use of Funds
- C. Historical Financial Statements
- D. Cash Flow Projections
- E. Pro Forma Income Statements
- F. Breakeven Analysis

IV. Appendices

There is also a sample business plan in Appendix B.

Remember, this is a suggested outline and probably contains much more than you need in your plan. If that's the case, simply omit sections in the plan which don't pertain. If you do omit parts, be sure to renumber the sections so they remain consecutive. Some people ask how long a typical plan should be. Naturally that depends on the nature of the business and the form of financing desired. For a simple acquisition, ten pages might do the job well. For a more complex business purchase, 100 pages or more may be needed to give all the necessary information.

BUSINESS PLAN—CONTENTS

Title Page. Look at the first page in the workbook, the blank title page. Notice the remark in parentheses. If you're going to have your plan typed directly from the workbook pages, be sure to scratch out any comments found in parentheses; they're meant only as clarifying notes for you.

Summary and Purpose. Next, examine the summary and purpose pages of your workbook. These two parts of the plan are optional. If your plan is relatively simple and straightforward, don't bother. If your plan is more complex, especially if it's going to be given to private investors, venture capitalists, or an SBIC (Small Business Investment Corporation), it's a good idea to include both a summary and a purpose. The summary is usually two to four paragraphs long and covers the items shown. Again, remember to remove all parenthetical comments prior to final typing. Use the purpose only if you're seeking equity (investment) financing from individuals or organizations who will be stockholders. A typical purpose statement reads:

> The purpose of this prospectus is to raise $30,000 in equity capital. Shares of stock in the XYZ Corporation are available at $10 per share, with 3,000 shares offered. Minimum investment is $2,000 (200 shares of $10 per share).

Sometimes the equity statement may be combined with a debt statement as well. If this were true in the example above, another sentence would be added:

> In addition, XYZ Corporation is seeking debt financing of $25,000 at currently existing commercial loan rates.

A word of caution about equity financing: get help from an attorney experienced in private stock offerings, a business consultant, an SBA management assistance officer, or a qualified banker. Securities laws are lengthy and they do change.

Table of Contents. See instructions in the workbook.

I. The Business

A. *Business Description*

1. Name. This is usually a one-liner like: "The name of the business is Imports Plus, Incorporated." Be certain, if the business is a corporation, to use the terms *Incorporated* (or *Inc.*) or *Corporation* (*Corp.*). If you're changing the name of the business, give the new name and its former name.
2. Location. Again, this is usually a simple statement like:

"The business is located at 3200 Front Street. Elkhart, Indiana."

3. Physical Facilities. Example: "Imports Plus, Inc., will lease 5,000 square feet of retail space at sidewalk level. Approximately 3,500 square feet are devoted to counters and shelves to display goods. The remaining 1,500 square feet contain a storeroom and an office."
4. Business History. This is optional, but you may want to briefly cover the history of the business, especially if there have been significant changes over the years. This section is more for outside readership—for example, a loan officer.

B. *Products or Services*

1. Description of Product Line. In this section you must describe what you plan to sell in such a way that any reader will understand your intentions. Because most small business purchases deal with what are called normal businesses (restaurant, clothing store, income tax service), these descriptions don't have to be too detailed. However, if you're buying a unique variation of a common business (a shop selling only women's sleepwear, a word processing service bureau) or plan to make significant changes in what the business sells, more detail is necessary.
2. Proprietary Considerations. Most financing sources look for the USP—unique selling proposition—of a business, and every business has one. It can be a patented product or something simple like location. For example, the USP of an ice cream and soda shop might be its location within a block of the junior high school. The USP of a neighborhood grocery store might be that it's the only one around that sells deli items. For some potential buyers, discovering the USP saves them a lot of money. When Steve Jacoby realized that what made Harry's Corner Bakery a success was Harry himself and not his location or his baked goods, Steve decided to look for a business with a less personal USP. Give this paragraph some careful thought; it's very important. You can always discover the USP of a business if you look carefully enough.

C. *Management Plan*

1. Organizational Form and Structure. If the business will be sole proprietorship and you're the proprietor with no employees, say so. If the business is to be a partnership, name your partners and designate their legal relationship (general or limited) as well as their financial relationship (amount of investment, percent of profits). If you plan to form a corporation, give the name of the state and the projected date of incorporation. There are times when no form is specified because the new, prospective owner wants to see which form investors prefer—limited partnership or stockholder—but this isn't common. Also, if you're buying a business that already has employees, draw an organization chart showing who does what and who they report to.
2. Résumés of Key People. Usually this is just yourself. Make the résumé easy to read—more like a biography than the stiff style used in job applications. Stress accomplishments and be sure to point out any past experience in the kind of business you're buying. Stick to facts and don't ramble. If you're not using outside financing, this section can be omitted.
3. Staffing Plan. This section applies only if you plan significant growth in the next three years. Think through how many people you'll need, when, how much you'll pay them, and the skills you want them to have.
4. Supporting Services. Give names of individuals and their firms and addresses. Eliminate any that don't apply.

D. *Operations Plan*

1. Facilities and Equipment. If you need to expand the description given in section I., A., 3., Physical Facilities, do it here. If you're buying a small manufacturing company, draw a floor plan. If you're going to need equipment (lathes, computer, deep-fat fryers), list what you'll need in addition to what's already there.
2. Plans For Growth and Expansion. Many new owners buy a very small business and then plan to expand it as time and capital permit. A small lunch counter may eventually become a full restaurant. A retail business such as a hardware store may evolve into a home center. If you plan to grow in the first three years, specify how this expansion will take place. Will you add more space? More products or services? Remember, physical growth—more space, more products, more sales—must be balanced by the staffing plan (I., C., 3.) and your financial projections (Section III).
3. Overall Schedule. Look ahead three years in the operation of the business. You have some choices here. What do you expect to accomplish in the next three years? Many times it makes sense to combine this schedule with the previous section on

growth and expansion. You can also do this part as a separate section, using a graphic approach or simply listing the events and approximately when they will occur.

4. Process Description. This section is normally used only for a manufacturing business to describe the process(es) by which goods are produced. If you're buying such a venture, it's important to tell the reader how your operation works. Sometimes a floor plan of the manufacturing (production) process, showing the flow of material and the individual operations, is included. If the business you're buying is something other than manufacturing, you can probably ignore this section unless you plan to operate in a unique manner, one quite different from your competition.

E. *Risks* (optional)

There is controversy over whether a section on the risks of a particular business should be included in a business plan. Some authorities suggest pointing out pitfalls weakens a business plan by bringing up negative factors. Others say it represents total honesty on the part of the prospective owner. If you're seeking equity funds, address the risks of the venture if for no other reason than the legalities of raising money by selling stock. If you accept equity and don't fully inform the investor of the nature of the investment, and the enterprise fails, that investor may sue for his or her money. If you specify the risks in the prospectus (the name for a business plan which is used to raise money), you usually absolve yourself from liability.

Only discuss unique and significant risks. Don't bring up such things as the possibility of fire or theft or storms; those are normal risks which all businesses face. Items that may be listed are

1. Selling to one small market segment.
2. Obtaining goods from a single supplier.
3. Being the first with a business idea.
4. Being in a technological field a large corporation could serve more easily.
5. Buying a business depending on rapid change in customer buying habits (high fashion, for example).

II. Marketing Plan

A. *Marketing Research*

1. Description of the Market. This section and the one to follow, Industry Trends, are often combined. If you decide to separate the two, use this section to describe the market for your goods and services in terms of
   a. the size of the market in annual sales, both nationally and locally;
   b. what characterizes that market: longstanding versus a new market (steel versus home computers, for example); how and why customers buy, the number of competitors; the ease of competitive entry into the market (service is generally easy, manufacturing difficult); special qualifications required by business owners (knowledge of accounting for a bookkeeping service); special problems and opportunities.
2. Industry Trends. We strongly suggest you consult periodicals as well as Department of Commerce's *U.S. Industrial Outlook* first; then discuss
   a. a brief history of the market as a whole—changes and growth rates.
   b. projections and forecasts for the market. For example, a study for a restaurant might show that the percentage of the food dollar spent on eating out is forecast to increase 0.4 percent per year.
   c. factors relating to growth (or decline). In the above example, one reason for the increase is the tendency for more people in a household to work. This results in more money to eat out and/or less time to prepare meals at home.
   d. the sensitivity of the market to external factors, like the state of the economy. For example, the sale of beer increases in tough times.
   e. local factors affecting your sales if your market is not national.
3. Target Market. Every small business and most large ones have a target market. It's important for you to know your target market so you can relate to the needs of those customers. You may be planning to target markets that the previous owner did not, and if so, describe these new markets. If yours is a consumer market, categorize your customers by geography, age, sex, income level and ethnic group. Also describe how and what this group buys relative to your business—a male teenager purchases more fad items with his allowance than a retired person with established wealth. Your market could be institutional—large businesses, machine shops in New Jersey, all hospitals, the federal government. Numbers are important. When one of us was in a medical electronics business, one of the target markets was physicians in

general practice. At the time there were 746,000 of them in the United States alone. Based on surveys we learned a $300 instrument could be sold to one-quarter of one percent of the general practitioners per year. Thus the annual estimated sales were

$$746{,}000 \times 0.0025 \times \$300 = \$559{,}500.$$

This section is also the place to discuss the results of any marketing research you conducted as part of your initial business analysis.

4. Competition. If you surveyed competitors, and we hope you have, this section is a piece of cake. Take a minimum of three competitors and discuss their strengths and weaknesses as you see them.

B. *Objectives and Strategy*

A simpler way to describe this section is "What I'm going to do and how I'm going to do it." The time period is three years with detailed attention given to the first year. Too many new business owners simply take over the seller's business with little or no thought how they're going to keep present customers and attract new ones. Naturally, your objectives (goals) and the various strategies to reach them come from your research. The more you know about your customers, their needs, and the competition's strong and weak points, the better the position you're in to plan your moves. There's no established format for this section; it can be done in prose form or it can be done as a table like the one below.

The more specific you are with strategies and objectives, the more measurable your results will be.

C. *Pricing Policy*

Most business owners set their prices by one or a combination of three basic ways.

1. By calculation: markup, gross margin, or return on investment.
2. As a result of the environment: competition, convention, government regulations.
3. As a marketing strategy: a very high price for a unique product (called skim-the-cream pricing), a very low price to gain market share (called penetration pricing), sale pricing.

Discuss how you plan to set your prices. It may be simple—100 percent markup on cost—or quite complex—beginning with high prices and successively lowering them as competition enters the market.

D. *Sales Terms*

This is usually pretty simple, and for many small businesses the terms are cash and carry. In addition, you may use bank credit cards (VISA, MasterCard), other cards (American Express, Diner's Club), or grant trade credit. If the latter is the case, specify payment terms: net 30 days; two percent to 10 days, net 30; and so on.

E. *Method of Sales and Distribution*

In most small businesses, the selling is done by the owner and there is no distribution. This might change in the second or third year, though, under your ownership. There are other forms of sales and distribution that can be used in more complex businesses. For example, the business may do its own distributing to its end customers and use sales clerks on the premises, have its own sales force calling on customers, or have independent sales representatives who take orders. Another form of internal distribution is mail order.

Objective	Strategy
Attain early income levels as shown in financial projections.	Open business with a sale to be announced in advance on radio and in local papers. Conduct sale for two weeks.
Increase profit from 5% to 7% after first six months.	Raise prices 11%; inform customers one month in advance.
Secure 20 new distributors in first six months.	Conduct mail campaign to potential distributors, using a mailing list.
Begin sales to U.S. government by second year.	Get on bidder's list during first year.
Build mailing list	Buy ad in *Yankee* magazine for 12 months.

External distribution means sales to an intermediary like a distributor or a dealer.

F. *Customer Service*

This may be non-existent for your business. This doesn't mean that you don't heed the concerns of your customers; customer service refers to things like a returns policy, moneyback guarantee or fulfillment of warranties. If you're going to sell appliances, for example, you may want to offer a repair service. If the present owner has instituted some unique forms of customer service (Remember our general store owner who put people's names on their Sunday papers?) be careful about doing away with them. You may lose those valuable customers.

G. *Advertising and Promotion*

What you must address here is:

1. Your means of communicating with your potential customers: newspaper, radio, magazines, direct mail, telephone.
2. The role of an ad agency if you plan to use one.
3. A timetable of media usage (radio and newspaper ads, each on a daily basis for the first six months), the scope of usage (4-inch by 4-column, 30-second spot), and its cost.
4. The basic message you're communicating, especially if you're using image advertising rather than advertising specific products or services.
5. Any promotion you have: opening day ceremony, press releases, appearance of some renowned person at your place of business, a balloon race that you sponsor.

H. *Forecasts*

In this section show your forecasts for the business for the first three years under your ownership. If you deal with one or just a few products, show the forecast by both units and dollars. Suppose you're going to sell two brands of small computers, one at $200 and the second at $600. Your sales forecast might look like this:

	Model A Units	($200) Dollars	Model B Units	($600) Dollars	Annual Sales in Total
Year 1	600	$120,000	100	$ 60,000	$180,000
Year 2	850	170,000	180	108,000	278,000
Year 3	1,000	200,000	225	135,000	335,000

If your business sells many products (a grocery store), simply show the total annual sales. These forecasts must come from *somewhere:* your marketing research or a projection of past performance. If they have thought and reason behind them, you can explain to a bank or an investor how the numbers were developed.

Also, the forecasts become an important factor in the section to follow—the financial data.

III. Financial Data

Before beginning these sections, please note we'll be using terms from accounting and finance—pro forma profit and loss, balance sheet, breakeven analysis. Because we'll give brief explanations but won't go into detail, we strongly suggest you spend the necessary time becoming totally familiar with these terms. To do this you can

1. Take a basic accounting course at your nearest college or vocational-technical school.
2. Spend time in the library reading books on small business finance. We like *Simplified Accounting For Non-Accountants* by Hayes and Baker (Wiley, 1980).
3. Obtain the book *Small-Time Operator* mentioned before, as well as these free or very inexpensive publications:
   a. "How to Read a Financial Report," available free from Merrill, Lynch, Pierce, Fenner & Smith, Inc., 165 Broadway, New York, NY 10080.
   It's excellent.
   b. A free listing of currently available reports is available from Small Business Reporter, Bank of America, Box 37000, San Francisco, CA 94137. These reports cost less than $5 each and although they change their offerings from time to time, are quite helpful. Some recent report topics include: "Financing Small Business," "Understanding Financial Statements," and "Cash Flow/Cash Management."
   c. Visit your nearest SBA office (see Appendix A) and ask for their free business planning material. Be certain to obtain the brochure on the

business plan for the kind of business you're buying. Currently, there are brochures available for four businesses: retail, service, construction, and manufacturing firms.

4. Have your accountant or a qualified business consultant explain terms and/or help you with any parts you don't understand.

Ready? Let's go.

A. *Proposal*

If you wrote a "Purpose" paragraph in the beginning of the plan, there's no need to repeat it here. If you didn't, state what funds you want to raise. Naturally if all outside financing is coming from the seller or you have enough resources to buy the business outright, it's not necessary to complete this section.

B. *Source and Use of Funds*

This information can be brief or lengthy depending on how the deal is structured. For most small acquisitions, though, it's usually simple and straightforward. For example:

Source of Funds

Buyer's down payment	$25,000
Seller financing	44,000
Short-term bank loan	10,000
	$79,000

Use of Funds

Purchase of business and assets	$40,000
Inventory	28,000
Improvements	5,000
Working capital	6,000
	$79,000

Note in our example that our buyer has chosen to make $5,000 in improvements and provide $6,000 in working capital (cash) to cover initial expenses like deposits (rent, utilities) and closing costs, as well as providing cash for payment of other obligations. You can't take over a business with nothing in your checkbook.

C. *Historical Financial Statements*

If available, the past three years' income statements and balance sheets from the business go here. If no statements are available, use the income tax returns.

D. *Cash Flow Projections*

This is the most important part of the plan. If done properly it demonstrates whether or not you can make a living from the business. Initially you must make assumptions about income and expenses in the future. The best way to do this is to look over monthly financial information from the previous operation. Notice how the sales change from month to month; see if there's a pattern; for example, high sales in November and December, low in the summer. Remember, you're looking into the future of the business under your ownership and you may be planning more sales.

Before you begin working with your detailed monthly information, you need to estimate the startup costs of the business and how much beginning cash you need. You can determine the amount of beginning cash by examining the available cash data given in the previous owner's monthly financial information.

Use the example below and the blank form in the workbook to record this information for your business.

STARTUP COSTS AND BEGINNING CASH

1. Inventory beyond that included in purchase price	$ —
2. Deposits	
a. Rent	500
b. Utilities, telephone	200
c. Sales tax	500
d. Other (specify):	—
3. Fees	
a. Professional (legal, accounting)	300
b. Licenses, permits, taxes	200
c. Other (specify):	—
4. Decorating, remodeling, repairs	1,000
5. Closing Costs	700
6. Insurance	400
7. Miscellaneous	500
TOTAL COSTS	$ 4,300
BEGINNING CASH	3,000

Remember, these are all one-time expenses that occur *before* you take over the business. If you have to buy more inventory before you open your door to the public, the amount spent for it becomes part of your startup costs. However, any inventory purchased *after* you open is *not* included here. Also note that two amounts—startup costs and beginning cash—are used in the cash flow projections. Let's continue our example, using the information from the startup costs and beginning cash form just completed. Our business acquisition is a small retail fabric store called Sew-N-Sew being purchased by Doris Macey. The full purchase price of the business is $48,000, including the inventory of $20,000. Doris' down payment to the seller is $15,000 and the seller is willing to finance the $33,000 balance at 12 percent interest for ten years. Using the table below showing monthly payments for each $1,000 borrowed, we find that a 12 percent interest rate for ten years yields a monthly payment of $14.35. To calculate her total monthly payment for the $33,000 loan, we multiply by 33:

$$\$14.35 \times 33 = \$473.55$$

Now we can begin working with the actual cash flow projection. Again, use the blank form in the workbook for your own projections. From the startup costs and beginning cash form we can see that Doris needs more money than her $15,000 down payment for the seller. In the first place she needs $4,300 to cover startup costs and another $3,000 for beginning cash. Although Doris might be able to finance this additional $7,300 either with the seller or a bank, we'll assume she has the funds herself. Keep in mind, then, that Doris needs a total of $22,300—the $15,000 down payment and an additional $7,300—to cover the startup costs and provide beginning cash. As you go through this material it may seem that we're saying the same thing in different ways or asking for a lot of numbers for your small business. However, keep in mind that we hope your small business is going to get bigger, and the bigger it gets, the more important it is to know where the money comes from and where it goes. It's a lot easier for Doris to do a cash flow projection for Sew-N-Sew now and keep updating it than try to pull those numbers together in five years when she has six employees and needs financing to build a new store. We've also constructed the cash flow projection in such a way that it provides the data that bankers, investors, accountants, consultants or other advisors may want to see. So even though it seems like a lot of work, by the time you're finished, you'll develop skills that will help you not only start your business, but also run it successfully.

Now let's look at Doris' monthly cash flow projection (see page 76). Notice she did the projection on June 16th with plans to begin operating the business in August. Looking at the entries for

MONTHLY PAYMENTS ON $1,000

Interest Rate	6%	8%	10%	12%	14%	16%	18%	20%
Years								
5	19.33	20.28	21.25	22.24	23.27	24.32	25.39	26.49
6	16.57	17.53	18.53	19.55	20.61	21.69	22.81	23.95
7	14.61	15.59	16.60	17.65	18.74	19.86	21.02	22.21
8	13.14	14.14	15.17	16.25	17.37	18.53	19.72	20.95
9	12.01	13.02	14.08	15.18	16.33	17.53	18.76	20.03
10	11.10	12.13	13.22	14.35	15.53	16.75	18.02	19.33
11	10.37	11.42	12.52	13.68	14.89	16.14	17.44	18.79
12	9.76	10.82	11.95	13.13	14.37	15.66	16.99	18.37
13	9.25	10.33	11.48	12.69	13.95	15.27	16.63	18.04
14	8.81	9.91	11.08	12.31	13.60	14.95	16.34	17.77
15	8.44	9.56	10.75	12.00	13.32	14.69	16.10	17.56

Notes: 1. For intermediate interest rates, use half the difference.
Example: 11% for 8 Years
12% rate: $16.25
10% rate: −15.17
$ 1.08 ÷ 2 = $0.54 + $15.17 = $15.71

2. Multiply loan in thousands of dollars to get actual payment.
Example: Loan of $27,500 for 10 years at 14%.
Table gives $15.53 for $1,000 loan.
Payment: 27.5 × $15.53 = $427.08

August we see she first shows her *total* investment as $52,300, which is the $48,000 purchase price plus the $4,300 startup costs. Next she lists the startup costs on line 2 and the purchase price on line 3. Now she shows her beginning cash of $3,000 in item 4. Her first month's (August) estimate of cash sales is $10,000 (item 5). Because she plans to run the business without granting credit to her customers, she has no accounts receivable (A/R, item 6). In item 7 Doris shows the seller's loan of $33,000 and in item 8 her down payment of $15,000. When items 4–8 are added together and the $48,000 in item 3 is subtracted from this total, the result is the total available cash for August, $13,000. This may seem like an unnecessarily complicated way to determine available cash, but in addition to providing data that is helpful in other areas, it keeps reminding you where that money comes from and where it goes.

Now let's describe the expense items, numbers 11–30:

11. Purchase of inventory. This is merchandise for resale or use in manufacturing. Note that Doris shows no expense for August because she already spent $20,000 for initial inventory which was included in the purchase price.
12. Employee wages. Base pay less taxes (including FICA). Notice Doris plans to bring a sales clerk aboard in November.
13. Payroll taxes and expense. This includes federal withholding, FICA (employee's and employer's portions), unemployment insurance, and benefits—health insurance, pension. This value can be 15–50 percent of item 12 plus item 30.
14. Outside services. Subcontracted work, janitorial service, trash pickup, snow removal. Don't include accounting or legal expenses.
15. Business supplies. Office supplies (paper, forms, file folders) and operating supplies (cleaning agents, lubricants, chemicals).
16. Repairs and maintenance. Self-explanatory. Includes painting.
17. Advertising. Include Yellow Pages cost. Notice that Doris increases advertising as Christmas approaches.
18. Car, delivery, travel. Some businesses lease or purchase a vehicle for delivery. Any travel and entertainment expenses also belong here.
19. Accounting and legal. Self-explanatory.
20. Rent. Please note that this is for real estate only; it doesn't include equipment rental.
21. Telephone. Self-explanatory.
22. Utilities. Heat, electricity, water.
23. Insurance. All business insurance: key person, liability, contents, workmen's compensation.
24. Taxes. Real estate taxes, inventory taxes, sales taxes, franchise fee (state fee for corporations).
25. Equipment. This is used for either outright purchases or for rental on such items as cash registers, postal meters, copiers, typewriters, computers.

26–27. Other. Note that Doris added a category for postage and printing.

28. Loan repayment. This is what Doris shows the monthly payment to the seller to be.
29. Miscellaneous. Small accounts including petty cash for which separate categories are not practical.
30. Owner's withdrawal. Doris plans to take out $1,400 a month until April when she gives herself a raise.

When Doris completes her expenses for August, she totals them in item 31 and subtracts the total expenses from the total available cash (item 9). This subtraction produces item 32, the ending cash for August, which is also the beginning cash for September.

The process of estimation continues month by month until one year is completed.

Take a look at item 32 for a moment, and notice that Doris' tightest month is March, when cash in the till is only $520. Given the fact that no projection can ever be totally accurate, she might want to either provide reserves or talk to a bank just in case March's sales aren't up to expectation.

Let's say you do a cash flow projection and discover ending cash keeps coming up negative, meaning your expenses keep outstripping your income. If that's the case, review your expenses and see if any can be reduced. Especially examine two critical items:

1. The loan repayment, which is called debt service. If you're borrowing too much money, possibly the business is overpriced or your down payment is too small. Also the terms of the loan may be such that the monthly payment is too high. If that's the case, you may have to reduce the interest, lengthen the term, or both. We discussed this in the previous chapter.
2. Owner's withdrawal. Do you want to take out more than the business can provide? If, after adjustments, the ending cash is still negative, don't proceed with the acquisition.

MONTHLY CASH FLOW PROJECTION

Name of Business: Sew-N-Sew

Address: Front St., Anytown

			1	2	3	4	5
		Year: 19XX-19X1					
		Month	Aug	Sep	Oct	Nov	Dec
1		Your investment	52300				
2	Less:	Startup costs	4300				
3		Purchase Price	48000				
4		Beginning cash	3000	3170	4980	4700	2060
5	Plus:	Cash sales	10000	14300	12700	15700	21000
6		Collection of A/R	–	–	–	–	–
7		Loans, other (specify)	33000	–	–	–	–
8		down payment	15000				
9	Total available cash		13000	17470	17680	20400	23060
10	Expenses						
11		Purchase of inventory	–	3760	5800	8700	11600
12		Employee wages	–	–	–	1000	1000
13		Payroll taxes & exp.	360	360	360	620	620
14		Outside services	80	80	80	80	80
15		Business supplies	300	300	350	200	500
16		Repairs and maint.	600	400	–	–	200
17		Advertising	950	800	900	1100	1100
18		Car, delivery, travel	500	600	500	700	800
19		Acctg. & legal	1200	800	100	200	200
20		Rent	500	500	500	500	500
21		Telephone	420	350	400	400	500
22		Utilities	280	300	350	400	470
23		Insurance	–	200	–	–	200
24		Taxes	200	–	–	200	–
25		Equipment	770	770	770	770	770
26		Other					
27		Postage & printing	1000	600	200	600	600
28		Loan repayment	470	470	470	470	470
29		Miscellaneous	800	800	800	1000	1000
30		Owner's withdrawal	1400	1400	1400	1400	1400
31	Total expenses		9830	12490	12980	18340	22010
32	Ending cash (9 less 31)		3170	4980	4700	2060	1050
33							
34							
35							

Prepared by: Doris Macey Date: June 16, 19XX

Line	Jan	Feb	Mar	Apr	May	Jun	Jul	Total 12 Months
1								
2								
3								
4	1050	1960	1410	520	2430	4290	2920	
5	11800	12300	15000	17600	18300	14700	13700	177100
6	–	–	–	–	–	–	–	–
7	–	–	–	–	–	–	–	33000
8								15000
9	12850	14260	16410	18120	20730	18990	16620	209590
10								
11	4000	5400	7700	7900	8100	7000	5900	75860
12	1000	1000	1000	1000	1000	1000	1000	9000
13	620	620	620	670	670	670	670	6860
14	80	80	80	80	80	80	80	960
15	100	150	100	100	250	300	100	2750
16	–	–	300	–	–	500	–	2000
17	300	400	500	600	650	650	500	8450
18	400	400	400	400	400	400	500	6000
19	–	–	200	–	–	300	–	3000
20	500	500	500	500	500	500	500	6000
21	270	300	350	400	450	450	300	4590
22	480	500	400	300	200	180	130	3990
23	–	–	200	–	–	200	–	800
24	–	200	–	–	200	–	–	800
25	770	770	770	770	770	770	770	9240
26								
27	100	260	300	300	400	300	500	5160
28	470	470	470	470	470	470	470	5640
29	400	400	600	600	700	700	700	8500
30	1400	1400	1400	1600	1600	1600	1600	17600
31	10890	12850	15890	15690	16440	16070	13720	177220
32	1960	1410	520	2430	4290	2920	2900	
33								
34								
35								

Well, if you made it this far, most of the work is done. The next sections of the business plan are optional but recommended. They take some effort, but nothing like the cash flow projections. Doing cash flow projections beyond the first year is not required but may be valuable. Many business owners do the second and third years by quarters. A blank form is provided in the workbook if you want to do this, and the sample business plan in Appendix B shows these later years.

E. *Pro Forma Income Statements.*

An income statement differs from a cash flow projection in that it's prepared for accounting and tax purposes. Pro forma simply means "in the future." We're not going to go into preparation in detail, but we want you to be aware of two major differences between income and cash flow statements.

1. An income statement doesn't show the total loan payment—it shows the interest portion of the loan because only that part is a deductible expense for tax purposes.
2. If you purchase a fixed asset—vehicle, computer, display case—you can't deduct the full cost of that asset; you can only *depreciate* a portion of it, and you must do that according to IRS guidelines, which can change.

Below is an income statement for Sew-N-Sew using figures from the 12-month total of the cash flow projection plus startup costs. The blank form in the workbook may be copied if you wish to do statements for more than one year.

Let's briefly describe how we obtained the figures for the pro forma income statement:

Net Sales. The annual cash sales of $177,100 are determined from the total in the cash flow projection. Because we show all other entries as a percent of sales, the $177,100 is represented as 100.0 percent.

Cost of Goods Sold. We used the amount of inventory purchases for the year (item 11, $75,860) here. This isn't totally correct because we should start with the beginning inventory, add the purchases for the year, and subtract the ending inventory. However, this value is close enough for our purposes.

PRO FORMA INCOME STATEMENT
Sew-N-Sew
(for the business year August 19xx to July 19xx)

			Percent
Net Sales		$177,100	100.0
Cost of Goods Sold		75,860	42.8
Gross Margin		$101,240	57.2
Expenses			
Payroll expense	$33,460		18.9
Outside services	960		0.5
Business supplies	2,750		1.6
Repairs and maintenance	2,000		1.1
Advertising	8,450		4.8
Car, delivery, travel	6,000		3.4
Accounting & legal	3,300		1.9
Rent	6,500		3.7
Telephone & utilities	8,780		5.0
Insurance	1,200		0.7
Taxes	1,500		0.8
Equipment rental	9,240		5.2
Depreciation	210		0.1
Postage & printing	5,160		2.9
Interest	3,860		2.2
Miscellaneous	9,700		5.5
Total Expenses		$103,070	58.2
Profit (Loss) before tax		$ (1,830)	(1.0)
Federal and state tax		—0—	—0—
Profit (Loss) after tax		$ (1,830)	(1.0)

Gross Margin. Net sales minus cost of goods sold.

Payroll Expense. This consists of

Owner's annual draw	$17,600
Employee wages	9,000
Payroll taxes and expenses	6,860
	$33,460

Outside Services. Same as cash flow.

Business Supplies. Same as cash flow.

Repairs and Maintenance. Same as cash flow.

Advertising. Same as cash flow.

Car, delivery, travel. Same as cash flow.

Accounting and legal

Initial	$ 300
For the year	3,000
	$ 3,300

Rent

Rent deposit	$ 500
Annual rent	6,000
	$ 6,500

Telephone & Utilities

Deposits	$ 200
Telephone	4,590
Utilities	3,990
	$ 8,780

Insurance

Initial	$ 400
Annual	800
	$ 1,200

Taxes

Initial	$ 200
Sales tax deposit	500
Annual	800
	$ 1,500

Equipment rental. Same as cash flow.

Depreciation. Your accountant can give you these values. In this instance, depreciation is 21 percent of the $1,000 remodeling charge, or $210.

Postage and Printing. Same as cash flow.

Interest
During the first 12 months, total payments on Doris' $33,000 loan (at 12 percent for ten years) are $5,680 (rounded off). Of that, $3,860 is interest and $1,820 is principal, reducing the loan balance to $31,180. You need a fancy calculator to determine this, or your banker or accountant can help you.

Miscellaneous

Closing costs	$ 700
Initial	500
Annual	8,500
	$ 9,700

Total Expenses. Self-explanatory.

Profit (Loss) before tax. Gross Margin less Total Expenses. Notice the business lost money from an accounting standpoint.

Federal and State tax. There is no tax due because of the loss.

Profit (Loss) after tax. Self-explanatory.

There's a blank form for a pro forma income statement in the workbook. If you want to do statements for more than one year, simply copy the form.

F. *Breakeven Analysis*

This is a simple calculation used to find the breakeven point for a business, that *theoretical* amount of dollar sales at which the business neither makes nor loses money.

If you plan to grow rapidly, you may lose money in the first year, and continue losing it into the second and possibly even the third year. There's nothing wrong with this as long as the plan shows (1) why there are losses, and (2) that there's a definite intent to make a profit eventually.

You can calculate the breakeven point in dollars of annual sales as follows:

$$\text{Breakeven} = \frac{\text{Fixed Costs (dollars annually)}}{\text{\% Gross Margin (expressed as a decimal)}}$$

What are "fixed costs"? These are items like rent that you pay whether or not you do any business. The simplest way to assess fixed costs is to use the total expenses from the income statement. This isn't exact because there are variable expenses like advertising, which aren't fixed like rent, interest or insurance, but are accurate enough. Let's look at a summary income statement:

		Percent
Net Sales	$200,000	100
Cost of Goods Sold	120,000	60
Gross Margin	$ 80,000	40
Expenses	100,000	(50)
Profit (Loss)	($ 20,000)	(10)

A banker or investor might want to know the breakeven point for this business, and it's *not* $220,000 ($200,000 sales plus the $20,000 loss). Using our formula of

$$\frac{\text{Expenses}}{\%\ \text{Gross Margin}}$$

$$\text{Breakeven} = \frac{\$100{,}000}{0.40} = \$250{,}000$$

and we can prove this by substituting our $250,000 net sales value:

		Percent
Net Sales	$250,000	100
Cost of Goods Sold	150,000	60
Gross Margin	$100,000	40
Expenses	100,000	40
Profit (Loss)	$ 0	0

You can see what happens: as sales rise to $250,000 and cost of goods sold stays at a *fixed* percentage (60 percent) of sales, but *increases* in dollar amount to $150,000 ($250,000 × 0.60), the expenses stay fixed at the same *dollar* amount of $100,000, which is a decreased (40 versus 50 percent) percentage of sales. All this makes the profit zero: the new business has broken even.

The space below is for you to figure the breakeven point for Sew-N-Sew. HINT: Go to the pro forma income statement.

IV. Appendices

This is not a place to throw a lot of extraneous material just to make the plan/prospectus look fat. Use it only for items that don't fit elsewhere:

- letters of intent from prospective customers.
- government contracts.
- photo of location.
- architect's plan.
- articles about the business.
- advertising materials.

SUMMARY

If you've worked along with us through all this explanation and now have the rough draft of your plan, you've done a magnificent job. Only about one business buyer in fifteen is doing what you've done. Congratulations!

In the next chapter we'll talk about banks and bankers—what they look for, what they like and don't like.

We'll also spend some time discussing other forms of financing as well as the role of the SBA. Armed with your completed business plan, you're in good shape to talk about financing.

Don't forget there is a hypothetical business plan in Appendix B to help you see what a completed plan looks like.

Chapter NINE

Small Business Financing

In this chapter we'll talk about the common forms of small business financing, especially bank loans. If you're paying cash for your business or getting financing from the seller, consider this background information. You may not need financing now, but as your business expands, or if you buy another one, you may eventually need some outside help. In any case, potential business owners need some idea about the different forms of financing available. But before we discuss loans (called debt), let's talk about equity, or the purchase of ownership.

FRIENDS, RELATIVES, AND OTHER INTERESTED PARTIES

If you don't have enough equity funds of your own to *leverage* a bank loan, you approach private individuals. What do we mean by leverage? Let's look at an example.

If you buy a new car for $10,000, you need some money of your own. Let's say the bank wants 20 percent down, or $2,000. If you have the two grand, that's your *equity* investment. The bank then loans you the $8,000. If you don't have the "downer," then you may have to go to Aunt Sadie to make up the difference.

Business purchases that don't involve seller financing work the same way. You need a "downer" before a bank will even talk to you. How much do you need? The answer depends on several factors—type of business, amount of collateral available, business conditions—but the range is 25 to 40 percent of the total needed. Most bankers won't go for a deal where the debt-to-equity ratio is greater than 2:1. This means you need to have at least one-third (33⅓ percent) of the total funds in the form of equity.

Let's look at another example. Suppose the economy is a bit tight and your local commercial bank tells you they won't consider your business purchase unless the debt-to-equity ratio is 1.5:1 or less. Let's also assume you need a total of $25,000 to buy the business. Therefore, if

$$\frac{\text{debt}}{\text{equity}} = 1.5$$

and

$$\text{debt} + \text{equity} = \$25{,}000$$

by substituting, we see

$$\begin{aligned} 1.5 \text{ equity} + \text{equity} &= \$25{,}000 \\ 2.5 \text{ equity} &= \$25{,}000 \\ \text{exquity} &= \frac{\$25{,}000}{2.5} = \$10{,}000 \end{aligned}$$

and then because

$$\begin{aligned} \text{debt} &= \text{total needed} - \text{equity} \\ \text{debt} &= \$25{,}000 - \$10{,}000 \\ \text{debt} &= \$15{,}000 \end{aligned}$$

To double-check

$$\frac{\text{debt}}{\text{equity}} = \frac{\$15{,}000}{\$10{,}000} = 1.5$$

Therefore, the bank is willing to loan you $15,000 (60 percent of $25,000) of what you need if you come up with $10,000, or 40 percent. If you have $6,000 yourself, you need to raise the other four thousand from equity investments. Although you can get advice from your banker in advance, you should have your equity before going to the bank for additional financing.

Besides having friends and relatives as equity investors, talk to potential

- business associates
- employees
- customers
- suppliers

before you approach strangers.

Strangers willing to back you financially are usually men and women who are well off financially and looking for a *sound* investment. You can find out names of such potential investors from

- your banker
- your accountant and attorney
- the local chamber of commerce
- the local industrial development group
- an SBA representative
- your stockholder
- your insurance agent.

You can also advertise in newspapers, but be sure to check with your lawyer for the correct wording. There are securities laws enacted to protect folks from scams; you won't run afoul of these if you follow your attorney's advice and explain to potential investors just what they're investing in. Your business plan/prospectus usually satisfies the legal requirements for "informing an investor."

We're going to discuss the corporate form of equity (buying stock) as opposed to the partnership form of equity (limited partners) because it's more common. When you take in equity, you usually sell ownershares of common stock. What happens when you sell common stock?

- you sell ownership
- you provide your stockholder(s) with a stock certificate or other proof of ownership
- you give your stockholder(s) voting privileges, usually one vote for each share of common stock.

How do you place a value on the stock of a very small business? You get the advice of your accountant and your attorney. What you're selling is an investment opportunity. Although dear Aunt Sadie wants to help you because you're her favorite niece, she must be shown what happens to her investment if the business succeeds or fails.

Let's go back to our example where you have $6,000 and need $4,000 in outside equity. Let's say Aunt Sadie is your outside stockholder and you each purchase stock at $1 per share. You then own 6,000 shares and your aunt 4,000. Because you have 60 percent of the votes and she has 40 percent, you have what is known as the controlling interest; that is, you own more than 50 percent of the corporation. It is *generally* a good idea to maintain this control because if you don't, you can be voted out of your own corporation.

How can we make this $4,000 a good investment for Aunt Sadie? Some people think they'll pay dividends on the stock, but that's extremely rare in small business. In the first place, the business needs every bit of cash it can use. Secondly, dividends come under what's known as double taxation; they're taxable to the corporation *and* the recipient. What you'll probably do is buy out Aunt Sadie when

1. the business grows and has several profitable years under your management;
2. the business can afford to do so either through the accumulation of a reserve fund or by borrowing.

Maybe in five years the value of Aunt Sadie's (and your) stock goes from $1 to $3 a share. If you and your aunt have the proper legal agreement, you pay her $12,000 for her 4,000 shares. She triples her money in five years. Not bad! When you buy her out, you then own 6,000 shares, or 100 percent, of the corporation. Aunt Sadie's stock returns to the corporation and becomes treasury stock, that which was once issued and is now repurchased. It sits in the *treasury* and can be re-issued without changing the bylaws.

If you can't buy out Aunt Sadie, she remains a stockholder until something happens. That "something" could be her death, in which case you might have to satisfy her heirs. Maybe they want cash and not some green certificate with naked people on it. Or that something could be the sale of the business. In any case, you need legal assistance. Your lawyer may suggest restricted stock; Aunt Sadie might be a sweet person who doesn't understand business, but you don't want her selling her stock to some sharpie who's only going to be a lot of trouble to you. If you sell her restricted stock, she signs an agreement not to sell her stock, or at least to give you first right of refusal, if she gets an offer to sell.

If you need to go beyond the Aunt Sadies of the world, you'll wind up talking with individuals who are fairly knowledgeable about business. Here are some guidelines for you:

1. If you're asked a question and don't know the answer, say so. Don't fumble through. Tell the person you'll get the information for them as soon as possible.
2. The really good investor certainly wants a return on his or her investment, but usually understands risk.
3. More than at the business idea, investors will look at you. Successful *people* run successful businesses.
4. If one or several of these potential investors seems to be something other than honest and forthright, back off.

You may want to hold an open meeting at the local Holiday Inn to present your business opportunity to a number of people at one time. There's nothing wrong with this or with putting an ad in the paper to announce your meeting. If you do it this way, be sure you

- don't make any outrageous claims like saying this is the investment opportunity of a lifetime
- don't use any approach that looks like a Florida land sale
- have copies of your business plan available for all
- have your attorney, accountant, and banker at the meeting
- make the presentation. Your advisors can help clarify certain technical points, but it's *your* show
- are honest. If you discuss opportunity, also discuss risk.
- have charts or other visual aids to help make major points.

One other valuable consideration is the creation of an escrow account for stockholder investments. Your attorney will probably tell you it's not a good idea to start spending your stockholders' money before all the financing is in place. Because one reason you're using equity is to leverage a bank loan, open an escrow account (preferably at the bank you hope to do business with) for these funds so your stockholders' money can be returned to them in full if you fail to secure the loan.

BANKS AND BANK FINANCING

Few books on small business financing spend much time on commercial lending and lending practices. Others try to teach you how to outwit or even bully a banker, painting the banker as uncaring, stingy, and stupid. We admit there are lousy bankers, just as there are lousy business owners and buyers; but if you approach a bank with the attitude you must beat the money out of them, you're going to have a rough time indeed. Commercial banks (usually the ones with "National" in their names) make most of their money from sound business loans. Of course they want that loan secured by collateral, but they don't want to go after that security in the case of default. They don't *want* your business, your house or your car; that's a hassle for them and they're never certain they'll get their money back. They want the loan repaid *in accordance with its provisions.* That's only fair to them, and it's the best deal for you as well. If the loan has fixed payments over some period of time, you plan that as a fixed cost of running your business. No other cost you have stays that uniform.

We're going to examine what banks are looking for and what turns them off. Remember one thing: banks are run by people—they hope, they fear, they laugh, they cry. A banker probably worries about his checkbook balance or wants her children to succeed in school. They have their operating rules just as you have yours.

WHAT DO BANKS LOOK FOR?

A bank is a very special kind of creditor, always looking for the "six C's" of credit:

1. *Character.* Who's borrowing this money? Businesses don't borrow and repay money, people do. If you seriously ran afoul of the law; if you defaulted on past obligations; if your overall reputation is in question, you probably face an uphill battle. Bankers also assess you as a person—Do you seem to know what you're doing? Are you enthusiastic about your new business purchase? Do you demonstrate self-confidence?
2. *Cause.* What is the money being used for? What type of business? Every bank has its own list of no-nos. One kind of no-no pertains to how the money is used. You can't just borrow money, stick it in the corporate checkbook, and pay yourself some extravagant salary. Remember the source-and-use-of-funds part of the business plan? Banks understand that some money must stay in the form of cash, but most of it must go for the purchase of real things—renovations, equipment, inventory. The other no-no is the type of business. Although you may find some variation from bank to bank, most lending institutions stay away from
   a. Proposed purchase of a business with multiple locations. You're going to have a hard enough time running one business, never mind two or more.
   b. Too much of one thing. Banks prefer businesses with a diversified product line, a diversified market, or both.
   c. Fads. No one ever knows for sure whether something will catch on or die away, but if your business purchase looks transient, a bank will back off.
   d. High-risk businesses. This list changes from time to time but usually includes bars, gas stations, high fashion stores, and businesses involving independent trucking, real estate development, and building contracting.
   e. Any business which borders on the unethical or even the immoral. Bankers are a conservative lot by nature.
3. *Capacity.* This refers to the capacity of the borrower to repay the loan. In a small business, a person pays off the loan, not the business. When you work your loan repayment into your cash flow projections, you demonstrate how repayment fits in with income and other expenses. Most bankers feel the biggest borrowing shortcoming on the part of new business owners is the failure to answer the question, "How will this loan be repaid?"
   Because the loan repayment must be made from sales, most bankers ask how you arrive at your projected sales total. If your marketing research is sound, you have a ready, logical, defendable basis. However, you may also have to face the fact that there may be bankers who simply refuse to accept your figures.
4. *Collateral.* Unless you're related to J. Paul Getty, no bank will grant an unsecured loan for a business purchase. You must show how your loan will be secured (collateralized). This is most often done by using the assets of the business you're buying as collateral. Don't forget the business itself may already be encumbered by a first mortgage to the seller.
5. *Capital.* What is the net worth of the borrower? How much capital is the owner putting into the business? What other equity capital is being supplied? By whom?
6. *Conditions.* As you know, the economy is always changing. During the early 1980s, business loans were difficult to secure and interest rates were hovering around 20 percent. When credit loosens up, banks become more competitive, capital is easier to come by, and it's cheaper.

In addition to the "six C's," additional business considerations that help sway a bank are

- a demonstrated track record for the business. This is why we stressed the length of time the business has been in existence as well as how long the seller has been running it.
- established guidelines. Naturally, any well-established franchise (McDonald's, Pizza Hut) can point to a high degree of success because they're selling a proven management method, not just a clever way to make fast food.
- a guarantee over and beyond collateral. This could be a co-signer to your loan who is reasonably well off, or it could be a loan guarantor like the SBA.

What banks look for in the buyer is

- someone who's truly committed to and enthusiastic about the business. Good bankers can easily spot folks on an ego trip.
- a person who appears to be reasonable and logical. You don't have to be the resident genius, but you must demonstrate you know what you're talking about.
- experience. There are two kinds of experience: business knowledge (general knowledge about how to

run *any* small business) and a background in the type of business you're buying (the ins and outs of this *particular* business). Having neither probably dooms your loan approval. One is fine; both are great! Financial experience is especially prized.

Things that *absolutely* turn a bank off include

- a poor personal credit history. This doesn't mean simply missing a payment here and there. However, if you've had a car repossessed, a mortgage foreclosed, or have been through business or personal bankruptcy, it's going to be tough. On a lesser scale, judgments against you or liens on any of your personal assets can also cloud the issue.
- a criminal record. Of course, the nature of the crime and nature of the sentence, if any, do enter in. It's one thing if you were detained in the slammer for one night for some domestic issue but quite another if you embezzled bank funds.
- no cash. If you have no equity whatsoever, either personal or invested by others, forget it.
- an "encumbered" business. If the business you're buying has had lawsuits, repossessions, and liens, few bankers will approve the loan.

GETTING READY TO GO TO THE BANK

Your preparation for your meeting with a commercial loan officer is more important than the actual meeting itself. Bankers tell us they're appalled by the number of people who wander in off the street without an appointment, with little or no preparation, and ask for a business loan. This approach might work with a loan shark, but don't *ever* try it with a reputable bank. You'll get a quick and possibly not-so-polite refusal. Respect the banker and show him or her normal business courtesies.

If you don't already do business with a commercial bank, you need to select one to apply for your loan. Your accountant can suggest one or two; you can also ask other business owners for their recommendations. Pick your first choice and one or two backups. When applying for a loan, first obtain the name and title of the appropriate officer who handles commercial loans for business purchases. In very small banks this may be the president. In medium-size banks you'll probably be referred to one of the commercial loan officers, possibly even the head of a commercial loan department. In larger banks, it may be the manager of the branch bank nearest you. In some cases you may wind up with a junior officer, but it's important you deal with the designated person. If you jump the chain of command within the bank, you may harm your case right from the beginning.

Should you apply for a loan at more than one bank? "Shopping the loan" should be done only under certain conditions and then with great care. Bankers tell us that if you have "the deal of the century" you're probably well-advised to go to several banks *BUT* make sure you inform each banker about the others. When you have some phenomenal situation you can look for the most favorable terms and even engage in a little negotiating (notice we said negotiating, not holding an auction) between banks. However, when your situation is average or marginal, shopping only hurts. A banker's attitude is, "This deal isn't the most attractive, so why should I spend all the time processing the loan application if some other bank might take it? The heck with it."

The next step is for *you* (not your accountant and especially not your attorney) to call the proper person at the bank, introduce yourself, and briefly describe the proposed business purchase and the amount of money you need. Sometimes you may even be dealing with the seller's bank; if so, the banker will already be familiar with the business.

Once you get your appointment, *ask* the officer if it's all right to bring your accountant and/or partner (limit it to one if there are more) along. *DO NOT* bring your attorney, and *never* bring more than three people. Bankers tell us lawyers only muddy up the first meeting because they often zealously attempt to overprotect their client. Bankers have certain things they won't budge on and having a lawyer sit there arguing extraneous issues only slows the process, frustrates the banker, and costs you money to boot. It may also kill the deal.

Tell the banker you have a business plan, and ask what else you should bring. Bankers vary considerably on this. If this is the first meeting, it may just be a get-acquainted session or what one bank president calls "mutual seduction." Chances are, though, the banker may also want to see

- copies of your personal income tax returns for the past three years;
- insurance documents (life, casualty);
- some bank forms (filled out in advance) like a personal financial statement. The bank is especially interested in credit references and your social security number. (See the next two pages for a widely used form.)
- a list of collateral being offered, showing market values of personal assets like homes, stocks, bonds, or those of the business;

PERSONAL FINANCIAL STATEMENT

IMPORTANT: Read these directions before completing this Statement.

- ☐ If you are applying for individual credit in your own name and are relying on your own income or assets and not the income or assets of another person as the basis for repayment of the credit requested, complete only Sections 1 and 3.
- ☐ If you are applying for joint credit with another person, complete all Sections providing information in Section 2 about the joint applicant.
- ☐ If you are applying for individual credit, but are relying on income from alimony, child support, or separate maintenance or on the income or assets of another person as a basis for repayment of the credit requested, complete all Sections, providing information in Section 2 about the person whose alimony, support, or maintenance payments or income or assets you are relying.
- ☐ If this statement relates to your guaranty of the indebtedness of other person(s), firm(s) or corporation(s), complete Sections 1 and 3.

TO:

SECTION 1 - INDIVIDUAL INFORMATION (Type or Print)		SECTION 2 - OTHER PARTY INFORMATION (Type or Print)	
Name		Name	
Residence Address		Residence Address	
City, State & Zip		City, State & Zip	
Position or Occupation		Position or Occupation	
Business Name		Business Name	
Business Address		Business Address	
City, State & Zip		City, State & Zip	
Res. Phone	Bus. Phone	Res. Phone	Bus. Phone

SECTION 3 - STATEMENT OF FINANCIAL CONDITION AS OF ____________ 19 ___

ASSETS (Do not include Assets of doubtful value)	In Dollars (Omit cents)		LIABILITIES	In Dollars (Omit cents)	
Cash on hand and in banks			Notes payable to banks - secured		
U.S. Gov't. & Marketable Securities - see Schedule A			Notes payable to banks - unsecured		
Non-Marketable Securities - See Schedule B			Due to brokers		
Securities held by broker in margin accounts			Amounts payable to others - secured		
Restricted or control stocks			Amounts payable to others - unsecured		
Partial interest in Real Estate Equities -			Accounts and bills due		
see Schedule C			Unpaid income tax		
Real Estate Owned - see Schedule D			Other unpaid taxes and interest		
Loans Receivable			Real estate mortgages payable -		
Automobiles and other personal property			see Schedule D		
Cash value-life insurance-see Schedule E			Other debts - itemize		
Other assets - itemize					
			TOTAL LIABILITIES		
			NET WORTH		
TOTAL ASSETS			TOTAL LIAB. AND NET WORTH		

SOURCES OF INCOME FOR YEAR ENDED ____________, 19 ____	
Salary, bonuses & commissions	$
Dividends	
Real estate income	
Other income **(Alimony, child support, or separate maintenance**	
income need not be revealed if you do not wish to have it	
considered as a basis for repaying this obligation)	
TOTAL	$

CONTINGENT LIABILITIES	
Do you have any contingent liabilities? If so, describe	
As indorser, co-maker or guarantor?	$
On leases or contracts?	$
Legal claims	$
Other special debt	$
Amount of contested income tax liens	$

PERSONAL INFORMATION
Do you have a will? ________ If so, name of executor.
Are you a partner or officer in any other venture? If so, describe.
Are you obligated to pay alimony, child support or separate maintenance payments? If so, describe.
Are any assets pledged other than as described on schedules? If so, describe.
Income tax settled through (date) ____________
Are you a defendant in any suits or legal actions?
Personal bank accounts carried at
Have you ever been declared bankrupt? If so, describe.

(COMPLETE SCHEDULES AND SIGN ON REVERSE SIDE)

SCHEDULE A - U.S. GOVERNMENTS & MARKETABLE SECURITIES

Number of Shares or Face Value (Bonds)	Description	In Name Of	Are These Pledged?	Market Value

SCHEDULE B - NON-MARKETABLE SECURITIES

Number of Shares	Description	In Name Of	Are These Pledged?	Source of Value	Value

SCHEDULE C - PARTIAL INTERESTS IN REAL ESTATE EQUITIES

Address & Type Of Property	Title In Name Of	% Of Ownership	Date Acquired	Cost	Market Value	Mortgage Maturity	Mortgage Amount

SCHEDULE D - REAL ESTATE OWNED

Address & Type Of Property	Title In Name Of	Date Acquired	Cost	Market Value	Mortgage Maturity	Mortgage Amount

SCHEDULE E - LIFE INSURANCE CARRIED, INCLUDING N.S.L.I. AND GROUP INSURANCE

Name Of Insurance Company	Owner Of Policy	Beneficiary	Face Amount	Policy Loans	Cash Surrender Value

SCHEDULE F - BANKS OR FINANCE COMPANIES WHERE CREDIT HAS BEEN OBTAINED

Name & Address Of Lender	Credit In The Name Of	Secured Or Unsecured?	Original Date	High Credit	Current Balance

(USE ADDITIONAL SCHEDULES IF NECESSARY)

The information contained in this statement is provided for the purpose of obtaining, or maintaining credit with you on behalf of the undersigned, or persons, firms or corporations in whose behalf the undersigned may either severally or jointly with others, execute a guaranty in your favor. Each undersigned understands that you are relying on the information provided herein (including the designation made as to ownership of property) in deciding to grant or continue credit. Each undersigned represents and warrants that the information provided is true and complete and that you may consider this statement as continuing to be true and correct until a written notice of a change is given to you by the undersigned. You are authorized to make all inquiries you deem necessary to verify the accuracy of the statements made herein, and to determine my/our creditworthiness. You are authorized to answer questions about your credit experience with me/us.

Signature (Individual) ______________________

S.S. No ______________ Date of Birth ______________

Signature (Other Party) ______________________

S.S. No ______________ Date of Birth ______________

Date Signed ______________________ 19______

- the personal financial statement of anyone acting as co-signer or loan guarantor;
- relevant certificates (incorporation or partnership agreement);
- past financial records of the business you're buying;
- a list of investors (stockholders, limited partners) showing amounts of investment.

Be certain to allow enough time to do this homework before the appointment.

There are two more things to do before the meeting. One is to be sure of your attitude. Be positive about the outcome of the meeting (even if you don't get the loan), your business purchase, and most of all, yourself. Remember, you're presenting a situation that's mutually profitable to you and the bank, monetarily and otherwise.

The second thing is to be sure your presentation is clear, logical, and concise. Don't memorize a "pitch," but think through what you want to say. You'll be asked probing questions like

- What makes you think this business will make it under your ownership?
- What will you do if a new competitor opens up?
- Why have you chosen this particular business to buy?
- Who are your employees? Suppliers? Customers?
- What business experience do you have? General business experience? In this particular kind of business?

THE MEETING ITSELF

It's the big day! You're going to meet a person whose dual dedication is to (1) help people in small business, and (2) maintain the financial integrity of his/her bank. The balance must exist for the bank or the bank ceases to exist. If you've done your homework, the meeting will be a piece of cake, and you're miles ahead of most others competing for the bank's money. Be certain to dress for the occasion: conservative clothes.

Remember, *you* make the presentation. If your accountant is present, he or she can answer questions but shouldn't make any lengthy discourse.

After the presentation and any questions, one of three things happens:

- you're turned down;
- you're asked to provide more information;
- you're told the bank will consider the deal.

If you're turned down, it may be the best advice you could get. You have the right to ask two questions:

1. Why was I turned down?
2. What do I have to do to get the loan?

Listen carefully to both answers. By all means, don't walk out in a huff. Thank the banker honestly for his time and advice and either look for another bank or begin making the necessary changes.

If you're asked for more information (detailed résumé, loan application form, financial data), tell the banker when he or she can expect to have it. There is a sample of a typical business application form on the next two pages.

If you're told to wait, ask when you can expect a final answer. The normal time is two weeks, but it could take longer for the bank to check your personal background and analyze your proposal. If the analysis is satisfactory, your proposal is presented at the weekly meeting of the loan committee. The decision of that committee depends on

- the past history of the business;
- the soundness of your proposal;
- any data the bank has generated studying your proposal;
- conditions in the local economy;
- the number of loans outstanding, especially in your kind of business;
- the bank's cash position;
- current government policies on loans.

If all is positive, you get your loan. A truly professional banker may suggest additional financing, either an increase in the loan or a line of credit, which is an already approved loan you don't use unless you need to.

There are some bankers who still think it's necessary to talk someone down on a loan. This isn't the same as an honest banker who analyzes your cash flow projections and finds errors either in your judgment or arithmetic and tells you your loan request is excessive. We're speaking of those asking for an arbitrary reduction for no sound reason. Don't go for this; it can only spell disaster for your business. If your business plan is done carefully, it shows what you need; taking less will only cause the business to fail. You're not haggling over a used car.

If you're turned down after the analysis period, again ask why and what needs to be changed. If you're approved, it may be conditional, which means

APPLICATION
Small Business Term Loan

TO: THE FIRST NATIONAL BANK OF ANYTOWN. Date ....

The undersigned hereby submit(s) application for a loan in the net amount of

.... Dollars $ [ ]

For the purpose of ....

....

....

to be repaid in .... monthly payments on the ☐5th ☐10th ☐15th ☐20th ☐25th ☐30th day of the month.

BUSINESS RECORD

☐ Corporation
☐ Partnership
Name of Business .... ☐ Proprietorship
(Please Print)

Kind of Business .... Phone No. ....

Address ....(Street)..................(City or Town)..................(Zone)..........(State)......

Year Business Established .... Annual Rent $ .... Lease Expires ....

Business Checking Account ....(Name of Bank)..

PRINCIPALS

Name .... Date of Birth ....

Residence ....

Residence Telephone No. .... No. of years at present residence .... Number of Dependents ....

Previous Residence ....

Checking a/c (bank) .... Title of account .... Balance $ ....

Savings or Cooperative a/c (bank) .... a/c no .... Balance $ ....

Real Estate Owned .... Date Purchased .... Mtge. held by ....

Cost $ .... Valuation $ ..... Original Mortgage $ ..... Present Balance $ .... Monthly Payments $ ...... Rental Income $ ....

Life Insurance: Face Amt. Carried $ .... Cash Value $ .... Subject to Loan of $ ....

Other Assets: Securities Mkt. Value $ .... Auto (Make & Year) ....

Open loans To Whom Owed	Original Amount	Unpaid Balance	Monthly Payment	Collateral
....	$	$	$	... .
....	$	$	$	... .

Name .... Date of Birth ....

Residence ....

Residence Telephone No. .... No. of years at present residence ...... Number of Dependents ....

Previous Residence ....

Checking a/c (bank) .... Title of account .... Balance $ ....

Savings or Cooperative a/c (bank) .... a/c no .... Balance $ ....

Real Estate Owned .... Date Purchased .... Mtge. held by ....

Cost $ .... Valuation $ ..... Original Mortgage $ ..... Present Balance $ .... Monthly Payments $ ...... Rental Income $ ....

Life Insurance: Face Amt. Carried $ .... Cash Value $ .... Subject to Loan of $ ....

Other Assets: Securities Mkt. Value $ .... Auto (Make & Year) ....

Open loans To Whom Owed	Original Amount	Unpaid Balance	Monthly Payment	Collateral
....	$	$	$	....
....	$	$	$	....

Borrower, in consideration of Bank making the loan to Borrower, hereby warrants, represents and agrees as follows:

1. If Borrower is a corporation, Borrower is duly organized and existing under the laws of.................... and is duly qualified as a foreign corporation in the States of ....

2. Borrower will cause the following present indebtedness of Borrower to be subordinated to the loan by a Subordination Agreement satisfactory to Bank.

Name of Creditor of Borrower	*Amount*
....	....
....	....
....	....
....	....

3. The execution, delivery and performance hereof and any security instruments or guarantees called for or delivered hereunder are (if Borrower is a corporation) within its corporate powers, have been duly authorized, are not in contravention of the terms of Borrower's Articles of Incorporation or By-laws or any amendment thereof and (whether or not Borrower is a corporation) are not in contravention of law or of any indenture, agreement or undertaking to which Borrower is a party or by which Borrower is bound.

4. All financial statements, profit and loss statements, statements as to ownership and other statements heretofore or hereafter given to bank in connection with this agreement are or will be true and correct subject to any limitation stated therein and Borrower is the owner of all property in which Borrower has given or is giving a security interest to Bank, free from all encumbrances and Borrower will so own all property in which Borrower hereafter gives a security interest to Bank.

5. Borrower will maintain executive personnel and management satisfactory to Bank.

6. Borrower will maintain adequate fire (including so-called extended coverage), public liability and other insurance as Bank may require, in such form and written by such companies as may be satisfactory to Bank and will upon request of Bank deliver to it the policies concerned. All policies covering property given as security for the loan shall have a loss payable clause in favor of Bank.

GENERAL INFORMATION

Has the business, or any of the principals ever been involved in any judgments, attachments or other legal proceedings other than divorce, custody, alimony or separate support proceedings?

☐ Yes ☐ No If "yes" attach memorandum giving details.

Name of Accountant:.. Tel. No. ....

Address: ....

Name of Insurance Agent:.. Tel. No. ....

Address: ....

The foregoing statements and any supplementary information are warranted by the undersigned to be true and are furnished to induce you to make the loan applied for, which, if made, will be used only for the purpose above stated.

The Bank is authorized to obtain from any source any information which it may require to enable or assist it to pass upon this application. If this application is approved, I also authorize the Bank to give credit information to others.

The undersigned knows that you rely and will continue to rely theron until written notice of any change therein is received by you. The undersigned will give you immediate written notice of any material change in the undersigned's financial condition, including any law-suit, begun or threatened, the effect of which may be to materially alter the said condition.

The undersigned will furnish you with such financial statements and data at such times and with such certifications as you may require, without expense to you. You, and your agents and accountants, may at any time inspect the undersigned's books and accounts.

This application shall remain in the property of the Bank, whether approved, not approved, withdrawn, or if the loan is paid.

Signed this day of , 19

It is unlawful to deny or stop credit or services or to damage anyone's credit standing because of his or her sex or marital status.

.... (SEAL)
Name of applicant

By ....
Title, if any

By ....
Title, if any

the bank may want something else, like an SBA guarantee. Other conditions can include

- more equity financing;
- more collateral or personal guarantees;
- a bit more homework.

FINAL STAGES

If you're totally approved, you go back to the bank to sign documents and discuss the final arrangements of the loan itself. See the following pages for a sample loan agreement and security (collateral) agreement. Your banker may suggest something other than a term loan on a fixed repayment schedule. You may hear words like variable interest rate, balloon payments, chattel mortgages. Be certain to ask questions about things you don't understand and be doubly certain you understand when payments are to be made, how much they are, what interest rate(s) you may be paying. We use the word *rate(s)* because the bank may propose one loan against inventory, another against real estate, a third against equipment, all with different interest rates and terms. Don't let this dismay you. The bank knows what it's doing. Below is a list of questions to ask before signing your name to anything.

CONTINUING BANK RELATIONS

Once you receive your loan, the worst thing you can do is never cooperate or communicate with your banker again. Bring all your business to that bank—personal checking, savings, certificates of deposit. You're involved in a total business deal. Don't shortchange the deal by spreading yourself around. You want someone on your side. Be certain to send quarterly income statements and balance sheets to your banker and plan to take her or him to lunch at least twice a year to share the good news as well as the bad. Your banker doesn't want to hear bad news on the street. If it looks as though you might need additional financing, advise your banker well in advance. Bankers never respond well to what is called "Friday night financing."

In addition, don't switch banks for a couple of percentage points on a loan. You'll only do it once. If you find after a year or so that the bank isn't giving you the service you want, then it's time to look for another one.

LOAN CHECKLIST

Questions to Ask the Loan Officer

1. Regarding interest—what rate is it? Is it fixed or variable? If it is variable, how much can it vary? When does the interest commence? Can I pay interest only for some period?
2. What is the maturity date of the loan? Is the last payment a normal payment or is it higher?
3. What is the price of placement? (NOTE: Some banks charge "points," meaning percentage points. This is a one-time fee. If you borrow $20,000 at two points—2 percent—you will be charged $400.)
4. Do I have the right to repay the outstanding balance at any time? Is there an additional fee if I do this?
5. Must I sign a personal guarantee for a business loan? (You will probably be required to do so.)
6. What will I be required to do other than make payments? (NOTE: You may have to maintain certain financial ratios or keep a certain minimum in your checking account, called a compensating balance.)
7. What insurance am I required to have?
8. Can the bank assign the loan to another party?
9. What am I restricted from doing (For example, paying dividends or high salaries)?
10. What constitutes default? What will happen? What costs will be charged? What is the process with foreclosure?

BUSINESS LOAN AGREEMENT

TO: THE FIRST NATIONAL BANK OF ANYTOWN.

The undersigned ____ (hereinafter called "Borrower") hereby applies to THE FIRST NATIONAL BANK OF ANYTOWN (hereinafter called "Bank") for a loan (hereinafter called the "loan") to be evidenced by a promissory note which includes the following provisions or such other provisions as to which Borrower and Bank may agree in writing:

Amount of Note: $______________________ Date of Note: ________

______________________________________, 19________

Payable: ____

Borrower, in consideration of Bank making the loan to Borrower, hereby warrants, represents and agrees as follows:

1. The business operations of Borrower are as follows: ______________ *(Insert type of business, i.e., machine shop, bakery, etc.)* and said business is a ______________ *(Indicate whether sole ownership, partnership, corporation or trust)*

2. Borrower will continue said business, will not engage in any other business without permission of Bank, and will use the proceeds of the loan only in connection with said business and for the following purposes:

3. Borrower's balance sheet as at ______________________

______ 19______ and the related statement of income and retained earnings for Borrower's fiscal year ending on such date, both of which have been delivered to Bank, are complete and correct and have been prepared in accordance with generally accepted accounting principles consistently applied throughout the period involved. There are no liabilities of Borrower contingent or otherwise not disclosed in said balance sheet and since the date of such balance sheet there has been no change in the assets, liabilities, financial condition or business of Borrower shown thereon other than changes in the ordinary course of business, the effect of which has not been in the aggregate materially adverse.

4. So long as any amount remains unpaid under the loan:

4.1 Borrower's current business assets will exceed Borrower's current business liabilities, both determined in accordance with generally accepted accounting principles consistent with those applied in preparation of the financial statements referred to in Paragraph 3, by at least ____

______ Dollars ($______________________). If left blank, this provision is not applicable.

4.2 Borrower's current ratio (the relationship of current assets to current liabilities) will be maintained at not less than   . Classification of current assets and current liabilities shall be computed in accordance with generally accepted accounting principles consistently applied.

4.3 Borrower's debt to tangible net worth ratio (the relationship of current and total indebtedness to tangible net worth) shall not exceed

For purposes of this Agreement, "tangible net worth" shall mean the aggregate book value of the assets of the Borrower (after deduction therefrom of all applicable reserves and allowances) minus (a) total liabilities, (b) any write-up in the value of assets occurring after the date hereof, and (c) all intangibles including but not limited to goodwill, leasehold improvements, patents, trademarks and the like.

4.4 Borrower's tangible net worth will not be less than $

4.5 Borrower will maintain compensating demand deposit account balances of at least ______________________________ of the outstanding loan balance. If such balances are not maintained, Borrower will be charged a deficiency fee equal in amount to the product of (X) the difference between the required compensating balance and the balance maintained, and (Y) the rate stated in the note of even date herewith for the number of days actually elapsed based on a 360 day year.

4.6 Borrower will furnish to Bank within ninety days after the close of each fiscal year of Borrower, a balance sheet of Borrower as of the close of such year and an income statement and statement of retained earnings for such year for Borrower (or if Borrower is an individual, for Borrower's business) certified by independent public accountants satisfactory to Bank; will furnish to Bank unaudited balance sheet and operating figures for each ______ ______________ within thirty days after the end of each of said periods, and such other data as Bank may request; and will at all times permit representatives of Bank to inspect and make extracts from Borrower's books and records.

4.7 Borrower will maintain its books and records relating to its financial affairs at all times in accordance with, and all financial statements provided for herein shall be prepared in accordance with, generally accepted accounting principles consistent with those applied in preparation of the financial statements referred to in Paragraph 3.

4.8 Borrower will not pay any dividends on any class of capital stock or make any other distribution or payment on account of or in redemption of capital stock, or permit any withdrawals from or distributions of the assets of Borrower, or if Borrower is an individual, the business assets of Borrower, except as salary or compensation for services rendered after the date hereof; provided, however, that total payment for services rendered (in cash or otherwise and including dividends, withdrawals, distributions, salary and compensation) in any month to the following may equal but shall not exceed the following amounts:

Name	Monthly Amount

4.9 Borrower will maintain financially sound and reputable insurers, insurance with respect to Borrower's properties and business against such casualties and contingencies and in such types and such amounts as shall be in accordance with sound business practices.

4.10 Without the prior written consent of Bank, Borrower will not:

4.10.1 Incur, assume or permit to exist indebtedness for borrowed money except from the bank.

4.10.2 Sell, factor or borrow on the security of Borrower's accounts receivable with or without recourse, guaranty, endorse (other than for collection or deposit in the regular course of business) or become or remain liable in respect of any indebtedness, obligation or liability of any other person, firm or corporation or permit any such secondary responsibility to exist.

4.10.3 Create or permit to exist any mortgage, pledge or other lien or encumbrance on any of Borrower's property except (i) those arising from attachments or similar proceedings, pending litigation, judgments or taxes or assessments whose validity or amount is currently being contested in good faith by appropriate proceedings and for which adequate reserves have been established and maintained in accordance with generally accepted accounting principles, or taxes and assessments which are not due and delinquent; (ii) liens of carriers, warehousemen, mechanics and materialmen and other like; (iii) pledges or deposits made in connection with workmen's compensation, unemployment or other insurance, old age pensions or other social security benefits, and good faith deposits in connection with tenders, contracts or leases to which Borrower is a party, or deposits to secure, or in lieu of, surety, penalty or appeal bonds, performance bonds and other similar obligations; (iv) encumbrances consisting of easements, rights of way, zoning restrictions, restrictions on the use of real property and similar encumbrances and minor irregularities in title; (v) landlord's liens under leases; and (vi) in favor of Bank.

4.10.4 Purchase or acquire any securities of or make any loans or advances to or investments in any person, firm or corporation except obligations of the United States government or any agency of the United States government or certificates of deposit issued by any one of the fifty largest banks in the United States.

4.10.5 Merge or consolidate or sell or dispose of all or a portion of Borrower's assets other than in the ordinary course of business, or in any way or manner alter Borrower's capital structure, including the sale, transfer or redemption of any shares of the Borrower.

4.10.6 Hire or discharge any officer or retain the services of any independent contractor or professional, except in the ordinary course of business and only where the management of the Borrower is not materially affected or changed.

4.10.7 In any twelve month period spend or become obligated to spend any sum in excess of ______________________________

Dollars ($______________________________) for the acquisition, construction or installation of properties to be carried in Borrower's books as fixed assets. If left blank, this provision is not applicable.

4.10.8 Incur or assume rental obligations for any current or future period of twelve consecutive months under leases of real or personal property aggregating more than $______________________________ or

aggregating more than $______________________________

________ at any one time outstanding.

5. The loan and any and all other obligations of Borrower to Bank, direct or indirect, absolute or contingent, due or to become due, now existing or hereafter arising (the "Obligations") shall at Bank's option become immediately due and payable without notice or demand at any time after (a) default in the payment or performance of any Obligation; (b) default in the observance by Borrower of any of the terms of this Agreement; (c) death, dissolution, termination of existence, insolvency, business failure, appointment of a receiver of any part of the property of, assignment for the benefit of creditors by, or the commencement of any proceedings under any bankruptcy or insolvency laws by or against Borrower or any party secondarily liable under any of the Obligations.

6. Any deposits or other sums at any time credited by or due from Bank to Borrower and any securities or other property of Borrower in Bank's possession may at all times be held and treated as security for payment of the Obligations. In the event any one or more of the events of default set forth in Paragraph 5 shall have occurred or be continuing, then regardless of the adequacy of any collateral, any deposits or other sums credited by or due from Bank to Borrower may be set off against any and all of the Obligations.

7. Borrower will at all times execute and deliver such further instruments and take such further action as may reasonably be requested by Bank in order to carry out the intent and purposes of this Agreement.

8. No failure or delay on Bank's part in exercising any right hereunder shall operate as a waiver thereof or any other right. No waiver hereunder shall be effective unless in writing and a waiver on any one occasion shall not be a waiver of any right or remedy on any future occasion.

9. In case of a default in the performance of the Obligations, Borrower will pay to Bank such further amount as shall be sufficient to cover the cost and expense of collection including (without limitation) reasonable attorneys' fees and expenses.

10. This Agreement shall be deemed to be a sealed contract under the law of (state) and shall be construed in accordance with such law.

11. Borrower agrees to additional provisions as follows:

____

____

____

____

____

____

____

____

____

____

IN WITNESS WHEREOF, Borrower has executed and delivered this Loan Agreement this ______________________________

day of ______________________________, 19______.

____

____

SECURITY AGREEMENT

____

NAME

____

STREET AND NUMBER CITY STATE

(hereinafter called "Debtor"), hereby grants to THE FIRST NATIONAL BANK OF ANYTOWN (hereinafter called "Bank"), to secure the payment of $______________________________ as provided in the Debtor's note(s) of even date herewith and also to secure the payment and performance of all other obligations of Debtor to Bank, whether direct or indirect, absolute or contingent, due or to become due, now existing or hereafter arising (all of the foregoing, including said notes, being hereinafter called the "Obligations"), a security interest in the following personal property of Debtor and any and all additions, substitutions, accessions and proceeds thereto or thereof (all of the same being hereinafter called the "Collateral"):

Debtor hereby warrants and covenants that—

1. The Collateral will be kept at ____ until such time as written consent to a change of location is obtained from Bank.

2. Except for the security interest granted hereby, Debtor is the owner of the Collateral free from all encumbrances and will defend the same against the claims and demands of all persons. Debtor will not pledge, mortgage or create, or suffer to exist, a security interest in the Collateral in favor of any person other than Bank, and will not sell or transfer the Collateral or any interest therein without the prior written consent of Bank.

3. The Collateral shall remain personal property irrespective of the manner of its attachment to any real estate. If the Collateral is attached to real estate prior to the perfection of the security interest granted hereby, Debtor will on demand of Bank furnish to Bank a disclaimer or disclaimers, signed by all persons having an interest in the real estate, of any interest in the Collateral which is prior to Bank's interest. Debtor will notify Bank in writing of any intended sale, mortgage or conveyancy of any real estate to which the Collateral is at any time attached, and will give written notice of the terms and conditions of this agreement to any prospective purchaser, mortgagee, grantee or other transferee of the real estate or any interest therein.

4. Debtor will immediately notify Bank in writing of any change in address from that shown in this agreement, shall at all reasonable times and from time to time allow Bank, by or through any of its officers, agents, attorneys or accountants, to examine, inspect or make extracts from Debtor's books and records, and shall do, make, execute and deliver all such additional and further acts, things, deeds, assurances and instruments as Bank may require more completely to vest in and assure to Bank its rights hereunder or in any of the Collateral.

5. Debtor will keep the Collateral at all times insured by such insurance as Bank may from time to time require, and in any event and without specific request by Bank, will insure the Collateral against fire, including so-called extended coverage, theft, and, in the case of any motor vehicle, collision, all insurance to be with such insurance companies as Bank shall approve, with loss thereon to be payable to Bank and Debtor as their respective interests may appear. All policies of insurance shall provide for not less than ten days' notice of cancellation or change in form to Bank and, if requested by Bank, shall be delivered to and held by it until all of the Obligations have been fully performed.

6. Debtor will keep the Collateral in good order and repair, and will not use the same in violation of law or any policy of insurance thereon. Bank may inspect the Collateral at any reasonable time, wherever located. Debtor will pay promptly when due all taxes and assessments upon the Collateral or for its use or operation or upon this agreement.

7. In its discretion, Bank may discharge taxes and other encumbrances at any time levied or placed on the Collateral, make repairs, thereof and place and pay for insurance thereon and pay any necessary filing fees. Debtor agrees to reimburse Bank on demand for any and all expenditures so made, and until paid the amount thereof shall be a debt secured by the Collateral. Bank shall have no obligation to Debtor to make any such expenditures nor shall the making thereof relieve Debtor of any default. Bank

may act as attorney for Debtor in making, adjusting and settling claims under any insurance covering the Collateral.

8. Debtor may have possession and use of the Collateral until default. Upon the happening of any of the following events or conditions, namely: (a) default in the payment or performance of any of the Obligations, of any liability or obligation to Bank of any indorser, guarantor or surety of or for any of the Obligations, or of any covenant or liability contained or referred to herein or in any note, instrument, document or agreement evidencing any Obligation; (b) any representation or warranty of Debtor in this agreement or made to Bank by Debtor to induce it to enter into this agreement or to make a loan to Debtor proving false or erroneous in any material respect; (c) loss, theft, material damage, destruction, sale, or encumbrance of or to the Collateral, or the making of any levy thereon or seizure or attachment thereof by legal process; (d) death, dissolution, termination of existence, insolvency, business failure, appointment of a receiver of any part of the property of, assignment for the benefit of creditors by, or the commencement of any proceeding under any bankruptcy or insolvency laws by or against Debtor, or any indorser, guarantor or surety of or for any Obligation; (e) such a change in the management or ownership of Debtor as in the opinion of Bank increases its risk; thereupon, and as long as such default continues, Bank may without notice or demand declare all of the Obligations to be immediately due and payable, and Bank shall then have in any jurisdiction where enforcement hereof is sought, in addition to all other rights and remedies, the rights and remedies of a secured party under the Uniform Commercial Code, including without limitation thereto the right to take immediate possession of the Collateral, and for the purpose Bank may, so far as Debtor can give authority therefor, enter upon any premises on which the Collateral, or any part thereof, may be situated and remove the same therefrom. Debtor will upon demand make the Collateral available to Bank at a place and time designated by Bank which is reasonably convenient to both parties. Bank will give Debtor at least five days' prior written notice of the time and place of any public sale of the Collateral or of the time after which any private sale thereof is to be made. From the proceeds of the sale, Bank shall be entitled to retain (i) all sums secured hereby, (ii) its reasonable expenses of retaking, holding, preparing for sale and selling, and (iii) reasonable legal expenses incurred by it in connection herewith and with such sale. No waiver by Bank or any default shall be effective unless in writing nor operate as a waiver of any other default or of the same default on another occasion.

9. Debtor waives demand, notice, protest, notice of acceptance of this agreement, notice of loans made, credit extended, collateral received or delivered or other action taken in reliance hereon and all other demands and notices of any description. With respect both to the Obligations and the Collateral, Debtor assents to any extension or postponement of the time of payment or any other indulgence, to any substitution, exchange or release of collateral, to the addition or release of any party or person primarily or secondarily liable, to the acceptance of partial payment thereon and the settlement, compromising or adjusting of any thereof, all in such manner and at such time or times as Bank may deem advisable. Bank shall have no duty as to the collection or protection of the Collateral or any income thereon, nor as to the preservation of rights against prior parties, nor as to the preservation of any rights pertaining thereto beyond the safe custody thereof. Bank may exercise its rights with respect to the Collateral without resorting or regard to other collateral or sources of reimbursement for liability. Bank shall not be deemed to have waived any of its rights upon or under the Obligations or the Collateral unless such waiver be in writing and signed by Bank. No delay or omission on the part of Bank in exercising any right shall operate as a waiver of such right or any other right. A waiver on any one occasion shall not be construed as a bar to or waiver of any right on any future occasion. All rights and remedies of Bank on the Obligations or the Collateral, whether evidenced hereby or by any other instrument or papers, shall be cumulative and may be exercised separately or concurrently.

10. This agreement and all rights and obligations hereunder, including matters of construction, validity and performance, shall be governed by the law of (state). This agreement is intended to take effect as a sealed instrument.

IN WITNESS WHEREOF, Debtor has executed ______________ original counterparts of this agreement on this ______________________________ day of ______________, 19____.

SIGNED AND SEALED
IN THE PRESENCE OF ______________________

*By*______________________

____
WITNESS

If things really get rough—sales are much lower than expected or expenses higher than you planned—your banker will want to see you monthly and have you do a cash flow projection. If you can't make a loan payment, for goodness sake, call your banker *in advance* and explain the situation.

If you get in trouble, your banker may help by

- restructuring the loan;
- postponing principal payments;
- granting more credit;

but only if you explain what's happened and show how you plan to correct the situation. Work with bankers and they'll work with you. They don't want to see you fail in business for several reasons:

1. It's often difficult for a bank to sell collateral and realize their investment from it.
2. A bank has expenses just as you do. If you can't meet your obligations, bank officers have difficulty meeting theirs.
3. If a smaller bank makes *one* business loan at their legal limit and that loan defaults, it alone may erase their entire year's profit.
4. It's a black mark on their record, too.

If you succeed, so do they. It's a nice partnership. Now let's talk briefly about the SBA.

THE SMALL BUSINESS ADMINISTRATION

The U.S. Small Business Administration is an agency of the government chartered specifically to help small business. Although the role of the SBA changes, it has two major purposes:

1. To provide education, information, and direct management assistance (consulting) at little or no cost.
2. To guarantee bank loans made to small business owners.

The SBA does loan some money, but this isn't the rule, and what little lending it does do may end soon.

If you want more information, visit your nearest SBA office (see Appendix A). Also read *How to Finance Your Small Business with Government Money: SBA Loans,* by R. Hayes and J. Howell (1980, John Wiley & Sons, NY).

THE SBA'S FINANCIAL ROLE: DIRECT LOANS

We mentioned that the SBA still makes a few *direct* loans but nothing like they used to. This is because by law, the agency may not make or guarantee a loan if a business can obtain funds on reasonable terms from a bank or other private source. A prospective business owner must seek private financing before applying to the SBA for a loan. You don't go to the SBA until you talk to the bank. If two banks turn you down,* *then* you can talk to the SBA about direct financing. However, the same criteria of personal resources, collateral, and a sound business plan still apply.

Although Congress may change the rules and the financial appropriations, the SBA has had some direct loan money available for

- low income and other disadvantaged persons;
- non-profit sheltered workshops;
- handicapped persons in business;
- firms engaged in certain specific energy conservation projects;
- development companies for projects aiding small businesses;
- export purposes.

To be eligible for an SBA loan, your business must

1. Meet certain size limitations (number of employees, sales).
2. Be independently owned and operated.
3. Be a profit-making venture (except for non-profit sheltered workshops).
4. Not be dominant in its field. (American Motors with 28,000 employees once qualified for an SBA loan using this provision.)
5. Not discriminate in its employment.

The SBA will not consider loans on speculative businesses, newspapers, and gambling operations.

As the loan applicant, you must

1. Be of good character.
2. Show an ability to run a business successfully.
3. Have enough personal capital at stake to withstand losses.
4. Show that the proposed loan is of such sound value or so secured as to reasonably assure payment.

Direct loans are presently limited to $150,000, except that handicapped assistance loans carry a maxi-

* This holds true in cities with populations greater than 200,000. You need only one refusal in smaller towns.

mum limit of $100,000. Regular business loans have a maximum maturity of 25 years, whereas working capital loans are generally limited to seven years. Interest rates vary with economic conditions.

Collateral must be one or more of the following:

1. A mortgage on land, building.
2. A mortgage on chattels. This is a lien against assets like cash registers and vehicles.
3. Assignment of warehouse receipts for marketable merchandise.
4. Guarantees or personal endorsements.
5. In some instances, assignment of current accounts receivable.

The SBA recommends the following steps for those wanting to buy a business:

1. Describe the type of business you plan to buy.
2. Describe your experience and management capabilities.
3. Prepare an estimate of how much you or others have to invest in the business and how much you need to borrow.
4. Prepare a current net worth statement (balance sheet) listing all personal assets and all liabilities.
5. Prepare a detailed projection of earnings for the first year the business operates under your ownership.
6. List collateral to be offered as security for the loan, indicating your estimate of the present market value of each item.
7. Take the foregoing material to your banker. Ask for a direct bank loan, and if you are declined, ask the bank to consider making the loan under the SBA's Loan Guarantee Plan. If the bank is interested in an SBA guaranteed or participation loan, ask the banker to contact the SBA to discuss your application. In most cases of guaranteed or participation loans, the SBA deals directly with the bank.
8. If a guaranteed or participation loan is not available, write or visit the nearest SBA office (see Appendix A). The SBA has 110 field offices which often send loan officers to visit many smaller cities if the need arises. To speed matters, make your financial information available when you first write or visit the SBA.

Notice your business plan already provides the proper information for the SBA.

THE SBA'S FINANCIAL ROLE: GUARANTEED LOANS

The guaranteed loan program is the one you'll most likely use if you go the SBA route. There are advantages and disadvantages to doing so. The advantages are:

- a bank *may* be more willing to make the loan with 70 to 90 percent of it backed by a government agency. If you receive a $50,000 loan which is 90 percent guaranteed by the SBA and you default, the SBA must fork over $45,000 to the bank and then come after you for reimbursement. The bank comes after the remaining $5,000 in a separate action.
- the loan guarantee sometimes permits a bank to do business differently, more flexibly. For example, some states don't allow banks to take second mortgages; with SBA participation, they can.
- the bank *may* be more willing to use a fixed interest rate—say, 2½ points over the prime interest rate—rather than a fluctuating one. The fixed rate is generally preferred by business owners because they can plan their interest expense in advance rather than have a constantly changing monthly interest bill.
- if you run into financial difficulty, the SBA may help re-negotiate the loan. As an agency of the U.S. government, the SBA has wide experience with small business, especially its problems. Sometimes a banker and a business owner disagree or even become hostile to one another and the SBA can act as a mediator between them.

Disadvantages are:

- some banks are reluctant to deal with the SBA; a few refuse outright.
- there's more paperwork, delays, and red tape, although the process has been greatly streamlined in recent years.
- because of politics, the SBA is often forced to change its methods and policies mid-stream.
- some SBA offices aren't as efficient or caring as others.
- most SBA employees and officers have no direct small business experience; they're career government employees who have never faced business risks.

BANKS, THE SBA, AND YOU

If all works properly, all three parties—the bank, the SBA, and you—benefit:

1. The *bank* gets the guarantee of the U.S. government for a majority of the loan. Bankers like to have two ways to get out of a loan (personal guarantees and business assets, for example) and some look for three. The SBA gives them one way out. Also the bank has an opportunity to make a better profit on the entire transaction. Bankers sell the guaranteed portion of the loan on what is known as the secondary market, get back most of the principal immediately, and collect a processing fee of a couple of

percentage points. The buyer of the guaranteed portion, usually a private individual, receives a U.S. government obligation.
2. The *SBA* fulfills its mission to help small business.
3. *You* get your money.

SUMMARY OF SBA PARTICIPATION

Remember, you don't have to use the SBA. If you can get your bank loan without it, you're better off in the long run because the SBA won't save you either time or money. However, if your banker recommends SBA participation, heed that advice and have patience with the procedure. Even if you're asked to do what you feel are silly things, remember what's at stake—your money and your business.

OTHER FINANCING SOURCES

Most small business purchases are funded by the buyer, the seller, a bank, and a few investors, who are usually friends and relatives. Although there are no statistics available, we estimate that 90 to 95 percent of the businesses get bought this way. The remaining 5 to 10 percent use other external sources. What's surprising is the number of other sources available.

COMMERCIAL FINANCE COMPANIES

You can find these institutions in the Yellow Pages under "Loans." Basically, a commercial finance company works with you just like a bank; they want the same documentation and collateral. Some of them are also approved SBA lending institutions. Because finance companies aren't regulated the same way banks are, they can legally take more risk. The default ratio on the amount of outstanding loans is higher, and therefore, so are the interest rates they charge. For this reason and several others, we're not in favor of them. Most aren't very professional in their dealings with small business owners. When you hear advertising like "no limit loans" and "money for any worthwhile purpose," it should make you wonder. The other problem with a finance company is that you're only a borrower to them. If you have a loan from a commercial bank and keep your business and personal accounts there, you're a total customer of that bank. If you run into a financial snag, your banker is going to be more flexible than a finance company.

STATE AND LOCAL DEVELOPMENT AUTHORITIES

Every state and practically every city with a population greater than 10,000 has some kind of development authority. State agencies (usually called economic development departments) won't be of much help to you as a small business owner because they're more interested in larger projects. However, your local authority may be of assistance, especially if you're buying a going concern employing more than one or two people. A book listing all state agencies as well as many other valuable sources is *The Insider's Guide to Small Business Resources,* by David E. Gumpert and Jeffry A. Timmons (1982, Doubleday & Co., Garden City, NY).

FARMER'S HOME ADMINISTRATION (FmHA)

There are 1,750 rural counties in the United States that have FmHA offices. Through their Business and Industry Loan Program, the FmHA guarantees bank loans much like the SBA but with a few differences:

1. Priorities are given to truly rural businesses.
2. The major test used by FmHA is whether the business provides real benefits to the community where it's located. These benefits include more jobs and/or attracting money from outside the community—tourism, for example.

If you plan to buy in a rural area, check your phone book listing under U.S. Government—Agriculture Dept. Because FmHA's ground rules change from time to time, it's a good idea to call before visiting them.

CUSTOMERS

If your venture is perceived as a good business by your customers, they might want to invest. Another method of financing is to have customers pay in advance; however, this must be handled very carefully or you may lose them as customers completely.

SUPPLIERS

Again, they may want to invest, but a more common route is the use of trade credit. You may find some suppliers willing to extend credit for 30 days and even longer, but it's more likely you'll have to pay cash for your first orders. If you don't ask, though, you'll never know.

EMPLOYEES

If you're going to sell stock to employees, be sure to check with your lawyer first. You may unwittingly create an ESOP—Employee Stock Option Plan—and that has legal ramifications. If you simply plan to borrow money from them, the loan is a standard business loan.

MISCELLANEOUS SOURCES

Some other interesting sources can be found if you look around. Small foundations exist to give financial aid to people buying small businesses and many of these are restricted to people of a particular ethnic group, geographic location, or even place of birth. Take the time to ask around. Also contact the professional trade association(s) which serves your type of business.

Other sources to consider are

- venture capitalists*
- local stock investment clubs
- credit unions
- savings and loan associations
- college endowment funds
- charitable trusts
- tax-exempt foundations
- large employers in your town.

Ultimately, of course, the most important source of financing for your business is the profit it produces.

SUMMARY

If you've done all we suggested, all that's left is the closing and taking over your new business. Although anti-climactic, the closing is an important meeting because all the paperwork is handled. Let's see what you can expect from this final formal meeting with the seller, the person who used to own your business.

* For a more lengthy description of venture capital, see Brian R. Smith's *Raising Seed Money For Your Own Business* (1984, Lewis Publishing Company).

Chapter TEN

The Final Stages

PREPARATION FOR THE CLOSING

All the loose ends of the business purchase are settled at the closing. Sometimes this meeting will occur only between the seller and you; in other cases there may be a roomful of people: buyer, seller, spouses, attorneys and accountants representing both sides, a broker, a banker, the landlord, and maybe even a candlestick maker or two. Because tax laws can become complex and because you might unwittingly create liabilities for yourself, it is important that you get some outside advice. What you want from the closing is

1. Protection from future liabilities created by the seller.
2. Assurance that what you're buying is free and clear of encumbrances, liens, mortgages—in other words, "good title" to the business.
3. A favorable tax basis for yourself.

The seller also wants favorable tax treatment as a result of the sale, and in addition, wants to be free of the business and its liabilities; and if granting financing, he or she wants security for that loan.

Again, because tax laws are not only complicated but change from year to year, we suggest you consult an accountant about their effect on your purchase. Keep in mind that choosing to buy a business without getting tax advice may create liabilities for yourself and the business.

Another item to consider is the seller's agreement not to compete. We know of a restaurant sold without this clause as a part of the final agreement. The seller, a famous chef in his own right, opened a new restaurant right across the street and nearly crippled his former business. Generally, such agreements restrict the seller from entering the same or similar businesses within a certain geographic limitation (radius of 25 miles for example) for a specified period of time (five years). This agreement can be given a financial value and made a part of the purchase price; that is, the price of the business is determined between you and the seller, but a certain portion of that price is allocated to a non-compete agreement.

Remember, it's important that as much of the purchase price as possible be allocated to assets. This can be a major tax advantage to you because you can take depreciation expense for assets; you can't do this with goodwill.

Once you and the seller reach an agreement and you approve the books, read the lease, and iron out any other details, it's time to set a date for closing the sale. Although the hard part may be over, some legal paperwork is necessary to change the ownership. You and the seller have to pick that all-important date—the date you want to take over the business and make it *yours*.

It's necessary to pick the date ahead of time because there are certain forms to be completed, signed, and in some cases filed with various governmental agencies. Bear in mind that, although the documents are roughly the same no matter where you live, the procedures may vary greatly depending on where the business is located. Procedures can also vary depending on whether a broker, attorneys, or just you and the seller are handling the sale.

The closing involves tying up all of the loose ends and, if properly prepared for, ensures that everything is as it should be. First, remember the term *bulk sale*. All states have a bulk sale act or provision and when you and the seller comply with it, it ensures you that all the inventory you buy from the seller is, in fact, owned by the seller and free from encumbrances. In other words, you don't want to unwittingly assume any of the seller's debts. In western states, an escrow company or agent publishes a notice that the sale of a business is taking place. In most other regions of the country, the burden falls on you to notify creditors that the business is being sold. You or your attorney obtain the names of all people the business owes money to: suppliers, banks. They must be notified by registered mail that you are buying the business, and when and where the closing will take place. Notifying suppliers and creditors enables them to collect for bills incurred prior to your taking over the business. It's important that you remember the bulk sale provisions; you don't want to be stuck with any of the seller's bills after you take over. An escrow company or agent (if your states uses them) sees that this is done properly. If an attorney is handling the sale, he or she also makes sure the provisions of the bulk sale law are carried out for your protection.

Let's briefly go over some of the other documents to be aware of to complete an orderly closing of your sale. Make sure you have a complete and accurate list of all the equipment you're purchasing. Both you and the seller should approve this so there can be no disagreement as to what is included in the sale. If the paintings on the wall, the adding machine in the office, or the TV over the bar are included in the assets, put them on the list with appropriate serial numbers if present. Prepare this list when you and the seller agree on the price and terms so a misunderstanding doesn't occur at the closing. If a broker is involved in the sale, he or she usually prepares this list for you.

You also want an assignment of the lease, or a new lease if the landlord is providing one. An assignment is a simple document signed by the seller and the landlord giving you permission to take over the unused portion of the seller's lease; you need the landlord's O.K. to occupy the premises in which your new business is located. Again, an escrow agent, broker, or attorney handling the sale prepares this document and sees that it's properly handled.

If you assume any of the seller's debts (money owed to a supplier, for example), you will probably have to sign a promissory note for the amount owed. You also sign what is called a UCC (Uniform Commercial Code) form. The broker, escrow company, or agent may conduct a UCC search or employ someone to search the records to make sure there's nothing owed against the equipment. It's important that this be done and that you have a copy of the results prior to the closing; you don't want to take over a business and discover there's money owed for something like equipment or inventory which you've already paid for in the sale price. Both the promissory note and UCC form are similar to the mortgage you sign when you buy a house.

In most cases, when you finance part of the purchase price of a business with the seller, the security for that money is the equipment and the other assets of the business. Be a bit careful of the seller who wants a personal guarantee—your house or other assets to secure the loan. If the seller wants something other than the business assets, he or she may be concerned the business can't afford the payments you've agreed to make.

Make sure that the final inventory is taken prior to the closing. If the business doesn't have a lot of inventory, you and the seller can probably do it yourself, but if it has a large inventory, use an inventory valuation service. If a broker is involved, he or she usually makes sure the inventory is done.

Just before the closing make sure you get the necessary licenses for the operation of a business, and put the utilities and phone service in your name. Notify your accountant of the day of possession so he can make sure he has everything he needs to set up your books.

At the closing you receive a bill of sale, which is proof that you own the business and equipment. You also get an agreement of sale, a copy of the offer to purchase, purchase and sale agreement, or some other document outlining the terms of the sale that you and the seller executed earlier in your proceedings.

As a reminder, here's a checklist of items you complete prior to the closing:

- ____ Offer to purchase (purchase and sale agreement) signed by both buyer and seller.
- ____ Copy of the lease
- ____ Approval of seller's books and records
- ____ Date set for closing of the sale
- ____ Business plan
- ____ List of fixtures and equipment
- ____ Application made to state liquor agency (if appropriate)
- ____ Application made to franchise company (if appropriate)

THE CLOSING

The closing is a formal meeting at which the proper forms and paperwork are executed and money changes hands. Then both buyer and seller go their separate ways—the seller is out of the business and you're in. There's usually at least one other person present: an attorney hired to represent the transaction, a broker, or, in some of the western states, a representative of an escrow company. It's their job to see that all papers are signed and passed.

Below is a list of items or information you need for the closing:

- ____ Lease assignment, sub-lease, or new lease
- ____ List of fixtures and equipment signed by both buyer and seller
- ____ Balance of funds due the seller
- ____ Bill of sale
- ____ Note, security agreement, and assumption of existing debts or loans
- ____ A covenant not to compete (if appropriate)
- ____ Franchisor approval (if appropriate)
- ____ State liquor license approval (if appropriate)
- ____ Corporate resolution (if seller is a corporation)
- ____ UCC search at appropriate state agency to insure the seller has revealed all liens and debts against the fixtures and equipment
- ____ Bulk sale compliance
- ____ Pro-rated portions of rent and other items like fuel oil in the tank
- ____ Inventory list and valuation

Forms such as the bill of sale, UCC search, and bulk sale compliance can often be purchased at office supply stores. If you use an attorney, he or she will furnish these. Make sure you leave the closing with clear title to all you're buying as well as the keys to the business.

Here's another checklist to remind you of some of the things you must do when you take possession of your new business:

- ____ Contact utility companies: electricity, gas, water, sewer
- ____ Contact fuel supplier
- ____ Contact telephone company
- ____ Secure janitorial, waste removal, snow plowing services
- ____ Call Yellow Pages advertising
- ____ Secure business, occupancy, health permits
- ____ Secure insurance (as needed)
- ____ Provide information to accountant
- ____ Make necessary filings for business name, business form (proprietorship, corporation)
- ____ File for appropriate taxes—sales and use, unemployment (your accountant will help with these)

ONCE UNDERWAY

Naturally we can't tell you all the things you need to know to run a business, but if you want this kind of information in depth, we suggest *How To Prosper In Your Own Business,* by Brian R. Smith (The Lewis Publishing Company, 1983).

However, here is a list of guidelines for successful small business operation. Although you may choose to ignore any and all of these, our experience shows the more you follow them, the greater your probability of success:

- Know when to seek and use the services of outside professionals—accountants, attorneys, consultants (including SBA personnel), insurance agents, advertising people.
- Keep your financing sources informed of how you are doing.
- Maintain a constant awareness of your market and its needs. Satisfy those needs.
- Take calculated, moderate risks in accordance with business conditions and your intuition. Learn to trust the latter.
- Strive for appropriate quality in your goods and services.
- Develop your own management style. Review your entire business every three months for the first two years of operation. Make changes when necessary.
- Remember that successful businesses are run ethically.
- Keep abreast of information that will help you and your business. Read. Attend seminars or courses. Join one or two trade or professional associations; subscribe to trade or professional magazines.
- Be fair, honest, and consistent (most important!) with your employees. Keep them informed of what's going on. Strive to develop the business's purpose with your employees.
- Don't skim. Not only is it illegal, it can actually hurt the future sale price of the business.
- Do a yearly business plan. Set goals.
- Know your competition. Keep track of what they're doing.
- Fight the temptation to grow too rapidly. You could outstrip your ability to finance that growth.
- Don't take too much out of the business for yourself, especially during the first year or two, but don't make yourself a martyr, either. Remember, few owners succeed in downgrading their lifestyles.
- Analyze your location every year. Move if traffic begins to decline.
- Allow credit sparingly if at all.
- Move slowly for the first year.

Most of all, learn to cultivate the idea that you are a successful business person. Some people mistakenly believe that buying and operating a successful business make them successful. It doesn't work that way.

Successful people buy and operate successful businesses.

Offices of the SBA

Addresses and Commercial Telephone Numbers

Boston, Mass. 02110
60 Batterymarch Street, 10th Floor
(617) 223-3204

Boston, Mass. 02114
150 Causeway St., 10th Floor
(617) 223-3224

Holyoke, Mass. 01050
302 High Street 4th Floor
(413) 536-8770

Augusta, Maine 04330
40 Western Avenue, Room 512
(207) 622-6171

Concord, N.H. 03301
55 Pleasant Street, Room 211
(603) 224-4041

Hartford, Conn. 06103
One Financial Plaza
(203) 244-3600

Montpelier, Vt. 05602
87 State Street, Room 204
P.O. Box 605
(802) 229-0538

Providence, R.I. 02903
380 Westminster Mall
(401) 351-7500

New York, N.Y. 10007
26 Federal Plaza, Room 29-118
(212) 264-7772

New York, N.Y. 10007
26 Federal Plaza, Room 3100
(212) 264-4355

Melville, N.Y. 11747
401 Broad Hollow Road, Suite 322
(516) 752-1626

Puerto Rico & Virgin Islands 00919
Chardon and Bolivia Streets
P.O. Box 1915
(809) 753-4572

St. Thomas, V.I. 00801
Veterans Drive, Room 283
(809) 774-8530

Newark, N.J. 07102
970 Broad St., Room 1635
(201) 645-2434

Camden, N.J. 08104
1800 East Davis Street
(609) 757-5183

Syracuse, N.Y. 13260
100 South Clinton Street, Room 1071
(315) 423-5383

Buffalo, N.Y. 14202
111 West Huron St., Room 1311
(716) 846-4301

Elmira, N.Y. 14901
180 State Street, Room 412
(607) 733-4686

Albany, N.Y. 12210
99 Washington Ave., Room 301
Mezzanine
(518) 472-6300

Rochester, N.Y. 14614
100 State Street, Room 601
(716) 263-6700

Philadelphia, Bala Cynwyd, Pa. 19004
231 St. Asaphs Rd., Suite 646
West Lobby
(215) 596-5984

Philadelphia, Bala Cynwyd, Pa. 19004
231 St. Asaphs Rd., Suite 400
East Lobby
(215) 596-5889

Harrisburg, Pa. 17101
100 Chestnut Street, 3rd. Floor
(717) 782-3840

Wilkes-Barre, Pa. 18702
20 North Pennsylvania Avenue
(717) 826-6497

Wilmington, Del. 19801
844 King Street, Room 5207
(302) 573-6294

Baltimore, Towson, Md. 21204
8600 LaSalle Road, Room 630
(301) 962-4392

Clarksburg, W.Va. 26301
109 North 3rd St., Room 301
(304) 623-5631

Charleston, W.Va. 25301
Charleston National Plaza, Suite 628
(304) 343-6181

Pittsburgh, Pa. 15222
1000 Liberty Ave., Room 1401
(412) 644-2780

Richmond, Va. 23240
400 North 8th St., Room 3015
P.O. Box 10126
(804) 782-2617

Washington, D.C. 20417
1030 15th St. N.W., Suite 250
(202) 653-6963

Atlanta, Ga. 30309
1375 Peachtree St., N.E., 5th Floor
(404) 881-4943

Atlanta, Ga. 30309
1720 Peachtree Street, N.W.
6th Floor
(404) 881-4325

Birmingham, Ala. 35205
908 South 20th St., Room 202
(205) 254-1344

Charlotte, N.C. 28202
230 S. Tryon Street, Suite 700
(704) 371-6111

Greenville, N.C. 27834
215 South Evans Street, Room 206
(919) 752-3798

Columbia, S.C. 29201
1835 Assembly Street, 3rd Floor
(803) 765-5376

Jackson, Miss. 39201
100 West Capitol Street, Suite 322
(601) 969-4371

Biloxi, Miss. 39530
111 Fred Haise Blvd., 2nd Floor
(601) 435-3676

Jacksonville, Fla. 32202
400 West Bay St., Room 261
P.O. Box 35067
(904) 791-3782

Louisville, Ky. 40201
600 Federal Pl., Room 188
P.O. Box 3517
(502) 582-5971

Miami, Coral Gables, Fla. 33134
2222 Ponce De Leon Boulevard
5th Floor
(305) 350-5521

Tampa, Fla. 33602
700 Twiggs Street, Suite 607
(813) 228-2594

Nashville, Tenn. 37219
404 James Robertson Parkway
Suite 1012
(615) 251-5881

Knoxville, Tenn. 37902
502 South Gay St., Room 307
(615) 637-9300

Memphis, Tenn. 38103
167 North Main St., Room 211
(901) 521-3588

West Palm Beach, Fla. 33402
701 Clematis St., Room 229
(305) 659-7533

Chicago, Ill. 60604
219 South Dearborn St., Room 838
(312) 353-0355

Chicago, Ill. 60604
219 South Dearborn St., Room 437
(312) 353-4528

Springfield, Ill. 62701
One North, Old State Capital Plaza
(217) 525-4416

Cleveland, Ohio 44199
1240 East 9th St., Room 317
(216) 522-4180

Columbus, Ohio 43215
85 Marconi Boulevard
(614) 469-6860

Cincinnati, Ohio 45202
550 Main St., Room 5028
(513) 684-2814

Detroit, Mich. 48226
477 Michigan Ave.
(313) 226-6075

Marquette, Mich. 49855
540 W. Kaye Avenue
(906) 225-1108

Indianapolis, Ind. 46204
575 North Pennsylvania St.
Room 552
(317) 269-7272

Madison, Wisc. 53703
212 East Washington Ave., Room 213
(608) 264-5261

Milwaukee, Wisc. 53202
517 East Wisconsin Avenue, Room 246
(414) 291-3941

Eau Claire, Wisc. 54701
500 South Barstow St., Room B9AA
(715) 834-9012

Minneapolis, Minn. 55402
12 South 6th St.
(612) 725-2362

Dallas, Tex. 75235
1720 Regal Row, Room 230
(214) 767-7640

Dallas, Tex. 75242
1100 Commerce St., Room 3C36
(214) 767-0600

Marshall, Tex. 75670
100 South Washington Street
Room G-12
(214) 935-5255

Albuquerque, N.M. 87110
5000 Marble Avenue, N.E., Room 320
(505) 766-3433

Houston, Tex. 77002
500 Dallas Street
(713) 226-4343

Little Rock, Ark. 72201
320 West Capitol Ave., Savors Fed. Bldg.
(501) 378-5876

Lubbock, Tex. 79401
1205 Texas Avenue, Room 712
(806) 762-7466

El Paso, Tex. 79902
4100 Rio Bravo, Suite 300
(915) 543-7580

Lower Rio Grande Valley
Harlingen, Tex. 78550
222 East Van Buren Street
P.O. Box 2567
(512) 423-4530

Corpus Christi, Tex. 78408
3105 Leopard Street, P.O. Box 9253
(512) 888-3333

New Orleans, La. 70113
1001 Howard Avenue, 17th Floor
(504) 589-6686

Shreveport, La. 71101
500 Fannin Street, Room 5B06
(318) 226-5196

Oklahoma City, Okla. 73102
200 N.W. 5th Street, Suite 670
(405) 231-4301

Tulsa, Okla. 74103
333 West Fourth Street, Room 3104
(918) 581-7495

San Antonio, Tex. 78206
727 East Durango Street
Room A-513
(512) 229-6250

Austin, Tex. 78701
300 East 8th Street
(512) 397-5288

Kansas City, Mo. 64106
911 Walnut St., 23rd Floor
(816) 374-5288

Kansas City, Mo. 64106
1150 Grande Ave., 5th Floor
(816) 374-3416

Des Moines, Iowa 50309
210 Walnut St., Room 749
(515) 284-4422

Omaha, Neb. 68102
19th & Farnum St., 2nd Floor
(402) 221-4691

St. Louis, Mo. 63101
One Mercantile Center, Suite 2500
(314) 425-4191

Wichita, Kans. 67202
110 East Waterman Street
(316) 267-6571

Denver, Colo. 80202
1405 Curtis Street, 22nd Floor
(303) 837-5763

Denver, Colo. 80202
721 19th Street
(303) 837-2607

Casper, Wyo. 82602
100 East B Street, Room 4001
P.O. Box 2839
(307) 265-5266

Fargo, N.D. 58108
657 2nd Ave., North, Room 218
P.O. Box 3086
(701) 237-5771

Helena, Mont. 59601
301 South Park Avenue, Room 528
Drawer 10054
(406) 449-5381

Salt Lake City, Utah 84138
125 South State St., Room 2237
(314) 425-5800

Sioux Falls, S.D. 57102
101 South Main Ave., Suite 101
(605) 336-2980

Rapid City, S.D. 57701
515 9th St., Room 246
(605) 343-5074

San Francisco, Calif. 94102
450 Golden Gate Ave.
P.O. Box 36044
(415) 556-7487

San Francisco, Calif. 94105
211 Main Street, 4th Floor
(415) 556-7490

Oakland, Calif. 94612
1515 Clay Street
(415) 273-7790

Fresno, Calif. 93712
1229 "N" St., P.O. Box 828
(209) 487-5189

Sacramento, Calif. 95825
2800 Cottage Way, Room 2535
(916) 484-4720

Las Vegas, Nev. 89101
301 E Stewart, P.O. Box 7525
Downtown Station
(702) 385-6611

Reno, Nev. 89505
50 South Virginia St., Room 308
P.O. Box 3216
(702) 784-5268

Honolulu, Hawaii 96850
300 Ala Moana, Room 2213
P.O. Box 50207
(308) 546-8950

Agana, Guam 96910
Pacific Daily News Bldg., Room 508,
Martyr & O'Hara
(671) 477-8420

Los Angeles, Calif. 90071
350 S. Figueroa St., 6th Floor
(213) 688-2956

Phoenix, Ariz. 85012
3030 North Central Avenue
Suite 1201
(602) 241-2200

Tucson, Ariz. 85715
301 West Congress Street, Room 3V
(602) 762-6715

San Diego, Calif. 92188
880 Front Street, Room 4-S-29
(714) 293-5440

Seattle, Wash. 98104
710 2nd Ave., 5th Floor
(206) 442-5676

Seattle, Wash. 98174
915 Second Ave., Room 1744
(206) 442-5534

Anchorage, Alaska 99501
1016 West 6th Ave., Suite 200
(907) 271-4022

Fairbanks, Alaska 99701
101 12th Avenue, Box 14
Federal Bldg. & Courthouse
(907) 452-1951

Boise, Idaho 83701
1005 Main St., 2nd Floor
(208) 334-2200

Portland, Oreg. 97204
1220 S.W. Third Avenue, Room 676
(503) 221-2682

Spokane, Wash. 99210
West 920 Riverside Avenue
Room 651, P.O. Box 2167
(509) 456-5310

APPENDIX B

Sample Business Plan

Author's Note: The accompanying hypothetical business plan for Harry and Simone's Coffee Shop, Inc., shows the purchase of a business without outside financing. For this reason, certain sections of the plan have been omitted because the new owners are preparing the plan strictly for themselves and not for a commercial lender or outside investor.

Business Plan for Henry and Simone's Coffee Shop, Inc.

Prepared by: Harold S. Morrison
Date: November 15, 1985

TABLE OF CONTENTS

I. THE BUSINESS

A. *Business Description*

1. Name. The name of this business is Harry and Simone's Coffee Shop, Inc.
2. Location. The business is located at 125 Main St., Longmeadow, Illinois.
3. Physical Facilities. The coffee shop leases approximately 2700 square feet of commercial space. The buyers are assuming the remaining two years of a five-year lease from Town and Country Properties, Inc., which specifies a monthly rental payment of $1,000 including heat and utilities.
4. Business History. The business was started in 1958 as The Knotty Pine Luncheonette. The first owner, William Reilly, operated the business until his death in 1979. During those 21 years, the operation of the business changed little, staying open from 6:30 a.m. to 4:00 p.m. weekdays and 7:30 a.m. to 11:30 a.m. on Saturdays. The present sellers, Jim and Diane Kaufman, purchased The Knotty Pine from Mr. Reilly's estate late in 1979. In the six years the Kaufmans operated the business as "Jim and Diane's," they expanded the menu to include dinners and are now open from 6:30 a.m. to 8:00 p.m., Monday through Saturday. The Kaufmans are selling the business because they wish to return to Baltimore, where they were both raised.

B. *Products or Services*

At the present time the restaurant offers light breakfasts, lunches, and dinners. The food consists of basic items (bacon and eggs, sandwiches, casseroles) and the prices are kept low. There is no license to serve alcoholic beverages. Besides regular mealtime patrons, many people who work in downtown Longmeadow come in for coffee breaks during the day.

C. *Management Plan*

1. Organizational Form. Harry and Simone's Coffee Shop, Inc., became an Illinois corporation on November 1, 1985. Harry and Simone Morrison are the sole stockholders.
2. Staffing Plan. Mr. Morrison is general manager of the restaurant and is also in charge of the cooking. He is assisted by a short order cook on Tuesdays through Saturdays. Mrs. Morrison is in charge of the serving staff, which consists of eight part-time personnel who work various schedules. Mrs. Morrison is also the bookkeeper for the business.
3. Supporting Services
   a. Accountant: John Howard, CPA
Lemon St., Longmeadow
   b. Attorney: Eloise Shapiro, Esq.
Main St., Longmeadow

D. *Operations Plan*

1. Facilities and Equipment. Besides tables, chairs, dishes, and utensils, the following equipment is part of the business:

   1 walk-in cooler
   2 dispensing freezers
   1 soda fountain
   1 milk dispenser
   2 soda dispensing machines
   2 calculators
   1 refrigerated sandwich table
   1 grill
   1 double deep-fat fryer
   1 microwave oven
   1 stove with ovens
   2 pastry display cases
   2 coffee machines
   1 ice machine
   1 dishwasher
   2 desks with reclining chairs
   1 4-drawer file cabinet
   1 meat slicer
   1 check writer

   There is also an electronic cash register, which is leased from the NCR Corporation for $100 per month.
2. Plans for Growth and Expansion
   a. 1986—During the first year of operation by the new owners, the coffee shop will be open on Sundays from 7:00 a.m. to 1:00 p.m.
   b. 1987—During this year the business will expand into catering.
   c. 1988—It is anticipated that the present space will be too small and the owners will investigate expansion at the present site or a move to a new location.

II. MARKETING PLAN

A. *Marketing Research*

1. Description of Market. The patrons of the coffee shop are middle-class men, women, and children who live in the Longmeadow area, which represents a total population of 25,000 people. Employment in the area has been stable; Longmeadow's unemployment has classically been below the national average. Over the past ten years the population of the area

has grown at an average annual rate of 0.5 percent. Both median family income and per capita income are 10 percent above the national average.

2. Industry Trends. Americans are spending more of their income eating out. The research firm of Frost & Sullivan estimates that in 1963 people spent 23 percent of their food dollar eating out. That percentage has steadily increased over the years and is projected to reach 28 percent by 1986. Furthermore, the U.S. Department of Commerce states that the general picture for restaurants as a group is one of continued growth. The Bank of America in San Francisco sees the future of coffee shops and small family-style restaurants to be reasonably healthy. Although the fast-food franchises have their share of the market, most of their effects on the market have already been felt.
3. Target Market. About the only change in the target market for Harry and Simone's in 1986 will be the church-goers on Sunday. Otherwise, the coffee shop will serve the same clientele as before. As catering plans become a reality in 1987 and after, civic organizations, and large employers, as well as private individuals will be sought out as clients.
4. Competition. Longmeadow has its share of food franchises. Presently there are the following: Red Barn, McDonald's, Burger King, Pizza Hut, Papa Gino's, KFC. In addition, there are another 41 eating places in the area, which range from Veteran's Diner (a ten-stool, marginal operation) to St. Andrew's, an elegant restaurant with 350 seats. There are two other small restaurants on Main Street which are direct competitors to Harry and Simone's:
   a. Sweetree. This is a small eating place catering primarily to young people, ages 18 to 28. It is more of an evening establishment than Harry and Simone's.
   b. The Forge. This business is run by an elderly couple who have owned it for over 35 years. Its hours are limited, and the physical facilities are badly in need of repair.

B. ***Pricing Policy***

The general policy will be to maintain a median level of food prices based upon the low prices of diners and several fast-food franchises and the high prices of the larger establishments. As soon as possible, all food costs will be analyzed to assure no item or meal is being served at a loss.

C. ***Sales Terms***

All sales are cash; no credit will be allowed.

D. ***Advertising and Promotion***

Local media will be used. Two 30-second radio spots on the two Longmeadow radio stations will be aired daily. In addition, a weekly 6 x 6″ ad will appear in the Longmeadow *Record.* Initial ads will announce the Sunday hours.

E. ***Forecasts***

Sales for the next three years are forecast to be

Year	Sales	Percent Change, Previous Year
1986:	$208,400	5.3
1987:	$265,500	27.4
1988:	$305,500	15.1

III. FINANCIAL DATA

A. ***Proposal***

The price of the business is $80,000, which includes inventory. Harry and Simone Morrison are providing a down payment of $25,000 to the seller. The seller will allow the Morrisons to assume a loan originally granted by the seller's father in 1979. The loan was for $40,000 at 16½ percent for ten years with a monthly payment of $682.57. The remaining balance on the loan is $25,000. Additionally, the seller will grant second financing of $30,000 at 12 percent for 15 years with a monthly payment of $360.05. Thus, the total initial debt service is $1,042.62.

B. ***Source and Use of Funds***

Source of Funds	
Buyer's down payment	$25,000
Assumption of seller's note	25,000
Seller financing	30,000
Additional cash from buyer	6,500
	$86,500

Use of Funds	
Purchase of business	$80,000
Startup costs	4,000
Beginning cash	2,500
	$86,500

C. ***Historical Financial Statements***

Shown below are the income statements for the past three fiscal years (October 1–September 30)

	Fiscal Years 1983	1984	1985
Net Sales	$172,000	$177,000	$198,000
Cost of Sales	68,000	71,000	81,000
Gross Profit	$104,000	$106,000	$117,000
Expenses:			
Employee wages	29,900	31,000	33,600
Payroll taxes & expense	13,000	13,100	15,000
Supplies	1,900	3,400	2,700
Repairs & maintenance	1,300	600	1,100
Advertising	3,000	3,000	3,200
Car, delivery, travel	1,400	1,800	1,900
Accounting & legal	900	1,000	800
Rent & utilities	12,000	12,000	12,000
Telephone	1,000	700	900
Insurance	1,400	1,700	1,400
Equipment	1,200	1,200	1,200
Interest	5,400	4,800	4,300
Depreciation	5,100	6,100	5,700
Owner's compensation	21,000	21,000	24,000
Miscellaneous	1,000	1,000	1,800
Total Expenses	99,500	102,400	109,600
Profit (Loss) Before Tax	$ 4,500	$ 3,600	$ 7,400
Federal and State Tax	1,400	1,000	1,500
Profit (Loss) After Tax	$ 3,100	$ 2,600	$ 5,900

D. *Cash Flow Projection*

STARTUP COSTS AND BEGINNING CASH

1. Inventory beyond that included in purchase price	$ —
2. Deposits	
a. Rent	1,000
b. Utilities, telephone	100
c. Sales tax	—
d. Other (specify):	—
3. Fees	
a. Professional (legal, accounting)	400
b. Licenses, permits, taxes	200
c. Other (specify):	—
4. Decorating, remodeling, repairs	1,300
5. Closing costs	500
6. Insurance	—
7. Miscellaneous	500
TOTAL COSTS	$ 4,000
BEGINNING CASH	$ 2,500

MONTHLY CASH FLOW PROJECTION

Name of Business: Harry and Simone's Coffee Shop   Address: Main St., Longmeadow, IL

		Year: 1986 Month	1 Jan	2 Feb	3 Mar	4 Apr	5 May
1		Your investment	84000				
2	Less:	Startup costs	4000				
3			80000				
4		Beginning cash	2500	1600	2900	3400	3400
5	Plus:	Cash sales	13000	16000	17500	16200	17800
6		Collection of A/R	–	–	–	–	–
7		Loans, other (specify)	55000	–	–	–	–
8		down payment	25000				
9	**Total available cash**		15500	17600	20400	19600	21200
10	**Expenses**						
11		Purchase of inventory	4000	6000	6700	6200	7000
12		Employee wages	2800	2500	3000	2900	3000
13		Payroll taxes & exp.	1200	1100	1300	1200	1300
14		Outside services	–	–	100	100	–
15		Business supplies	–	100	200	100	200
16		Repairs and maint.	–	–	200	–	400
17		Advertising	500	400	500	600	500
18		Car, delivery, travel	100	100	100	200	100
19		Acctg. & legal	200	–	–	400	–
20		Rent	1000	1000	1000	1000	1000
21		Telephone	100	100	100	100	200
22		Utilities	–	–	–	–	–
23		Insurance	500	–	–	–	400
24		Taxes	–	–	500	–	–
25		Equipment	100	100	100	100	100
26		Other					
27		Vehicle purchase	–	–	–	–	–
28		Loan repayment	1100	1100	1100	1100	1100
29		Miscellaneous	300	200	100	200	100
30		Owner's withdrawal	2000	2000	2000	2000	2000
31	**Total expenses**		13900	14700	17000	16200	17400
32	**Ending cash (9 less 31)**		1600	2900	3400	3400	3800
33							
34							
35							

Prepared by: Harold Morrison

Date: November 15, 1985

Jun	Jul	Aug	Sept	Oct	Nov	Dec	Total 12 Months
3800	4500	400	2400	2400	3000	6000	
16500	16900	17400	18700	19000	20700	18700	208400
–	–	–	–	–	–	–	–
–	–	–	–	–	–	–	55000
							25000
20300	21400	17800	21100	21400	23700	24700	244700
6200	6500	6600	7600	7600	8000	7000	79400
2600	2700	2500	3100	3200	3600	3600	35500
1100	1300	1200	1400	1400	1500	1700	15700
–	100	–	100	100	200	300	1000
100	100	–	200	100	100	300	1500
–	–	–	200	100	–	600	1500
600	400	300	700	600	600	800	6500
100	100	100	200	100	100	200	1500
–	200	–	–	100	–	500	1400
1000	1000	1000	1000	1000	1000	1000	12000
200	100	100	200	100	100	200	1600
–	–	–	–	–	–	–	–
–	–	–	–	400	–	–	1300
500	–	–	500	–	–	500	2000
100	100	100	100	100	100	100	1200
–	5000	–	–	–	–	–	5000
1100	1100	1100	1100	1100	1100	1100	13200
200	100	200	100	200	100	200	2000
2000	2200	2200	2200	2200	2200	3000	26000
15800	21000	15400	18700	18400	18700	21100	208300
4500	400	2400	2400	3000	6000	3600	

CASH FLOW PROJECTIONS (Second and Third Years)

Name of Business: Harry and Simone's Coffee Shop Address: Main St, Longmeadow, IL.

Year: 1987

#			Qtr. 1	Qtr. 2	Qtr. 3	Qtr. 4	Year Totals
1							
2							
3							
4		Beginning cash	3600	5800	5400	2600	
5	Plus:	Cash sales	66000	61000	73500	58000	258500
6		Collection of A/R	–	–	–	7000	7000
7		Loans, other (specify)	–	–	–	–	–
8							
9	Total available cash		69600	66800	78900	67600	282900
10	Expenses						
11		Purchase of inventory	26000	24000	34600	23500	108100
12		Employee wages	12000	12700	14000	13700	52400
13		Payroll taxes & exp.	5000	5200	5600	5400	21200
14		Outside services	300	400	300	200	1200
15		Business supplies	500	400	600	400	1900
16		Repairs and maint.	600	100	700	200	1600
17		Advertising	2000	1700	2500	2200	8400
18		Car, delivery, travel	300	400	600	700	2000
19		Acctg. & legal	500	400	600	500	2000
20		Rent	3000	3000	3000	3000	12000
21		Telephone	500	500	600	500	2100
22		Utilities	–	–	–	–	–
23		Insurance	400	500	500	400	1800
24		Taxes	500	600	600	700	2400
25		Equipment	400	500	400	400	1700
26		Other					
27		asset purchase	1000	–	600	–	1600
28		Loan repayment	3300	3300	3300	3300	13200
29		Miscellaneous	500	500	600	500	2100
30		Owner's withdrawal	7000	7200	7200	7200	28600
31	Total expenses		63800	61400	76300	62800	264300
32	Ending cash (9 less 31)		5800	5400	2600	4800	
33							
34							
35							

Prepared by: Harold Morrison Date: November 15, 1985

Year: 1988

	Qtr. 1	Qtr. 2	Qtr. 3	Qtr. 4	Year Totals
	4800	9300	4300	8400	
	69000	68000	71000	63000	271000
	8500	7500	9000	9500	34500
	–	–	–	–	–
	82300	84800	84300	80900	332300
	32500	34700	31700	27800	126700
	14200	16000	15500	15700	61400
	5600	6200	6000	6100	23900
	300	300	300	300	1200
	500	500	500	500	2000
	100	400	1000	500	2000
	2000	2200	2500	2500	9200
	600	800	1000	1000	3400
	600	600	600	600	2400
	3000	3000	3000	3000	12000
	600	700	700	700	2700
	–	–	–	–	–
	500	500	500	600	2100
	700	700	800	800	3000
	400	500	400	400	1700
	–	2000	–	1800	3800
	3300	3300	3300	3300	13200
	600	600	600	600	2400
	7500	7500	7500	7800	30300
	73000	80500	75900	74000	303400
	9300	4300	8400	6900	

E. *Pro Forma Income Statements*

	Calendar Years					
	1986		1987		1988	
Net Sales	$208,400	100.0	$265,500	100.0	$305,500	100.0
Cost of Sales	79,400	38.1	108,100	40.7	126,700	41.4
Gross Profit	$129,000	61.9	$157,400	59.3	$178.800	58.6
Expenses:						
Employee wages	$ 35,500	17.0	$ 52,400	19.7	$ 61,400	20.1
Payroll taxes & exp.	15,700	7.5	21,200	8.0	23,900	7.8
Outside services	1,000	0.5	1,200	0.5	1,200	0.4
Supplies	1,500	0.7	1,900	0.7	2,000	0.7
Repairs and maint.	2,800	1.3	1,600	0.6	2,000	0.7
Advertising	6,500	3.1	8,400	3.2	9,200	3.0
Car, delivery, travel	1,500	0.7	2,000	0.8	3,400	1.1
Accounting & legal	1,800	0.9	2,000	0.8	2,400	0.8
Rent & utilities	13,000	6.2	12,000	4.5	12,000	3.9
Telephone	1,700	0.8	2,100	0.8	2,700	0.9
Insurance	1,300	0.6	1,800	0.7	2,100	0.7
Equipment	1,200	0.6	1,700	0.6	1,700	0.6
Interest	7,300	3.5	6,700	2.5	5,900	1.9
Depreciation	6,800	3.3	6,000	2.3	7,600	2.5
Owner's compensation	26,000	12.5	28,600	10.8	30,300	9.9
Miscellaneous	3,200	1.5	2,100	0.8	2,400	0.8
Total Expenses	126,800	60.8	151,700	57.1	170,200	55.7
Profit (Loss) Before Tax	$ 2,200	1.1	$ 5,700	2.2	$ 8,600	2.9
Federal and State Tax	500	0.3	1,600	0.6	2,000	0.7
Profit (Loss) After Tax	$1,700	0.8	$4,100	1.6	$6,600	2.2

F. *Breakeven Analysis*

$$1986:\quad \frac{\$126{,}800}{.619} = \$204{,}900$$

$$1987:\quad \frac{\$151{,}700}{.593} = \$255{,}800$$

$$1988:\quad \frac{\$170{,}200}{.586} = \$290{,}400$$